Student Study Guide

to accompany

Exceptional Lives
Special Education in Today's Schools

Fourth Edition

Rud Turnbull
Ann Turnbull
Marilyn Shank
Sean Smith

Prepared by
Jody S. Britten

Upper Saddle River, New Jersey
Columbus, Ohio

Vice President and Executive Publisher: Jeffery W. Johnston
Editor: Allyson P. Sharp
Development Editor: Heather Doyle Fraser
Editorial Assistant: Kathleen S. Burk
Production Editor: Sheryl Glicker Langner
Design Coordinator: Diane C. Lorenzo
Cover Designer: Ali Mohrman
Production Manager: Laura Messerly
Director of Marketing: Ann Castel Davis
Marketing Manager: Amy June
Marketing Coordinator: Tyra Poole

Pearson Prentice Hall™ is a trademark of Pearson Education, Inc.
Pearson® is a registered trademark of Pearson plc
Prentice Hall® is a registered trademark of Pearson Education, Inc.
Merrill® is a registered trademark of Pearson Education, Inc.

Pearson Education Ltd.
Pearson Education Singapore Pte. Ltd.
Pearson Education Canada, Ltd.
Pearson Education—Japan

Pearson Education Australia Pty. Limited
Pearson Education North Asia Ltd.
Pearson Educación de Mexico, S.A. de C.V.
Pearson Education Malaysia Pte. Ltd.

10 9 8 7 6 5 4 3 2 1
ISBN: 0-13-112602-4

Table of Contents

Preface

The student study guide for *Exceptional Lives: Special Education in Today's Schools, Fourth Edition*, has been written to support you in your mission to learn and to apply that knowledge to the educational setting in which you are preparing to work. In most cases this textbook is used for introductory courses. No matter if you are a general or special educator, the materials in this guide have been developed in efforts to push you to think critically and begin shaping your ideas, beliefs, and values as someone who will work individuals with disabilities in the years ahead.

It is easy to look at the textbook, the student study guide, or the embedded project ideas as just another set of materials that you *might* use someday. But as you will learn in the text, the opportunities for interaction with individuals with disabilities increase daily as our expectations for social inclusion become more commonplace. Whether you are striving to be a teacher, continuing your education, taking courses for licensure, or preparing for a related career, it is our belief that you will be able to apply your knowledge of this text to better understand not only your future or current students, but your neighbors and community members with disabilities as well.

This is not just material to be memorized, but rather material to be learned and understood. Each chapter goes to great lengths to personalize the story of a child with a disability, so that you can, at the least, read about the daily lives of individuals with disabilities or people whose lives have been impacted in one way or another by disabilities.

The Companion Website provides a comprehensive list of resources and is referenced continually throughout the *Student Study Guide*.

How to use the Student Study Guide

Chapter Overview
Each chapter overview provides a brief description of the chapter and offers specific learning objectives.

Instructional Goals
Concrete and measurable learning goals that should be achievable after your interaction with content in the text, the Companion Website, and the *Student Study Guide* are included in this section. These goals are also included in the PowerPoint slides as connections to the content being presented; check with your instructor to find out if they are using the PowerPoint presentations provided with the text.

Guiding Questions
Replacing the traditional outline, the guiding questions will provide an organized note-taking tool for you to use while reading the text.

Key Terms
Vocabulary specific to the chapter content is included as a guide for understanding. Understanding these key terms will help in your overall comprehension and ability to generalize terms to the environment in which you will one day work.

Case Study Summary and Focus Activity
Each chapter in the text provides one or more case studies of students with disabilities, their families, or their communities. These case studies are referenced here as a starting point to further discussion. Each case study in the text should be reviewed for comprehensive understanding. The information in the case study should be used to complete the focus activity that immediately follows the case study summary.

Artifact or Project Opportunities for Students
Within this section of each chapter, you are provided with a list of possible artifacts to support the application of the content presented in the text. Most options for application can be considered performance-based artifacts to demonstrate competencies for related professional standards.

Spot Check – Pre-Instructional Questions
The Spot Check provides a self-check so that if there are major gaps in your understanding, you will have questions prepared for class sessions.

Materials Available on the Companion Website
To ensure that you are aware of the information and materials available on the Companion Website, all materials are listed in this section of the *Student Study Guide*.

Questions and Reflections
This section allows room for you to take notes, refine questions, and prepare for discussions, exams, or assignments related to course content.

Standards/Topics – Project Alignment Matrix
New to this edition is the matrix aligning CEC professional standards, Praxis Standards, and INTASC principles with text content. Each chapter has an individual matrix that shows correlating chapter topics and related projects or artifacts. A comprehensive matrix aligning all standards and topics is available in the Appendix of the textbook. This is to be used to provide a context for your understanding of professional standards as well as to enable you to show competency in those standards through performance-based artifacts or projects.

Video and Audio Case Studies

As part of the *Exceptional Lives* Companion Website, audio clips have been made available for each of the 16 chapters. These clips feature the authors introducing specific chapter-based issues as well as tips on what to consider when reading the chapter. Pay close attention to how the authors tie the four major themes to considerations within individual chapters. To better understand parents and the issues they face raising a child with a disability, video clips have been produced featuring the parents from the chapter vignette. These short clips offer glimpses of their perspectives on collaboration, inclusion, meeting the diverse learning needs of their son or daughter, and how technology can play a role in the life of their child. As you watch these clips, listen to the efforts they have made to better the life of their child. As a future educator, consider ways you might interact with this parent to achieve success in the classroom for the child, his or her parents, and your entire class. The video/audio clips icon (seen above) will be placed intermittently in the Student Study Guide to remind you that these clips are available on the Companion Website.

 **Graphic Organizers**

Each chapter is presented with a Graphic Organizer available in the back of this guide and on the Companion Website in digital form. Each Graphic Organizer is designed to highlight the common components including definition/characteristics, identification/evaluation, curriculum/instruction, and teaching/collaboration. Utilizing the Graphic Organizer in class (during lecture, group work, or independent review) may support your understanding of the multiple levels encompassed by of the topics being discussed within each chapter. The filing cabinet icon is used to remind you that the Graphic Organizer would be a good companion to that topic or section.

Chapter 1
OVERVIEW OF TODAY'S SPECIAL EDUCATION

Chapter Overview

Disability affects nearly 15 percent of all infants, toddlers, children, and adolescents. Increasingly, teachers in today's schools are interacting with a variety of disabilities on a daily basis. As we progress into a new era of accountability with public education it is essential that classroom teachers understand the systems in which they work. Today's special education system is a complex web that involves many different stakeholders. In this chapter you will interact with a profile of special education in today's schools, be introduced to the different categories of disabilities, be provided with an overview of the characteristics of students with disabilities, and lay the foundation for understanding the Individuals with Disabilities Education Act and its related outcomes for students with disabilities.

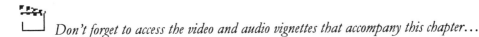 *Don't forget to access the video and audio vignettes that accompany this chapter...*

Instructional Goals

After reading this chapter you will be able to:
1. Understand the characteristics of special education in today's schools.
2. Connect individuality with disability in relation to categorization and characteristics.
3. Identify the categories of disabilities.
4. Describe the various stakeholders in special education.
5. Understand the basic components of IDEA.

Guiding Questions

Don't forget about the Graphic Organizer available on the Companion Website.

Who are the students with disabilities?

What is the total number of students served?

What are the age groups and gender of students served?

How many states require services for gifted education?

What are the categories of disability?

What are the effects of labeling on students with special needs?

What is "people-first" language?

What are the socioeconomic characteristics of students with disabilities?
How does the family education level interact with disability?

What are the racial and ethnic trends in special education?

What is disproportionate representation?

How are students underrepresented?

What roles do special education personnel have?

How is the support of paraprofessionals utilized?

What judicial decisions have impacted special education today?

What are the principles of IDEA?

What is zero reject?

What is an IFSP?

What is an IEP?

What is the least restrictive environment?

What other federal laws support individual needs of students?

What are the long-term goals of special education today?

Key Terms

In the space provided below, define the key terms in the chapter.

FAPE

IDEA

IEP

IFSP

Inclusion

LRE

Related Service Personnel

Zero Reject

Case Study Summary and Focus Activity

Case Study Summary

Nolan Smith is a two-year-old with Down Syndrome. Nolan is a very active toddler with a support system at home and in the community. Receiving services to support his development in several different areas, Nolan has a physical therapist, an occupational therapist, and a speech therapist who work to support him as often as once a week. Nolan's family has been open to allowing other individuals into their life to work with him and assist them in making the best decisions, choices, and long-range plans for their son. Nolan is most definitely an individual; he enjoys playing with his sister and brother, among others, and has his likes and dislikes. Nolan and the team of individuals who care about him are taking steps early on that will support him in becoming a member of the community, working and contributing to his livelihood, and even living with support on his own.

Focus Activity

Collaboration Connection...	Your Thoughts...
Who are some of the individuals you may collaborate with while working with a student with a disability?	
How will you as a teacher interact with the special education system of today?	
What were the effects of key judicial rulings on today's system of special education?	

Diversity Link...	Your Thoughts...
How can you as a teacher safeguard against overrepresentation of certain populations of students?	

Focus on Inclusion...	Your Thoughts...
How will the label of a specific disability alter your approach to working with individual children?	

Universal Design Application...	Your Thoughts...
How can universally designed learning support the goals of special education?	

Artifact or Project Opportunities

Focus on Curriculum and Instructional Choices:
Using the community map available on the Companion Website, choose one activity that you might be interested in implementing with a student similar to Nolan. Describe how you would facilitate that activity and list the materials or people from whom you would need support in order to facilitate the activity to its fullest potential. Link the activity to concrete skills that Nolan would develop as a result of the activity.

Focus on Technology:
As presented in the chapter, there are many resources and services available to students, families, and professionals working with the special education system. In order for you to develop a personal library of resources, develop a list of web-based resources that will help you to keep up with special education-related information such as legal, curricular, and advocacy issues. Upon compiling the list, write a brief description of each site and how teachers or other service providers could use it.

Focus on Collaboration:
Using the link available on the Companion Website, view the Circle of Inclusion resources. After completing the activity "Expanding the Circle," complete the questions, check your answers, and create a brief summary of the activity and the lessons learned. This activity will allow you to show that you are able to articulate the benefits of inclusion, understand how students with disabilities can be supported, and define keys terms related to inclusion.

Focus on Diversity:
Review the statistics on overrepresentation in the chapter. Using this as a basis for information read the article, "Creating Culturally Responsive, Inclusive Classrooms" by Winfred Montgomery, published in the Council for Exceptional Children's journal *Teaching Exceptional Children*, Volume 33, Number 4. The article is available online at http://journals.cec.sped.org (a direct hyperlink to the article is available on the Companion Website). After reading the article, write a brief reflection connecting the author's statements, the information provided in Chapter 2, and your opinions on how standards relate to the teaching and learning of students with exceptionalities.

 Spot Check

1. What are the trends with regard to the populations of students represented in special education?

2. Describe some of the concerns over labeling.

3. Identify one judicial ruling that affects the special education system in today's schools.

4. List the basic categories of disabilities.

5. What are the long-term outcomes underlying special education?

Questions and Reflections
(After reading the chapter, use this area to keep track of your questions or reflections)

⌗Standards/Topics – Project Alignment Matrix

The following professional standards are addressed in Chapter 1 within the correlating chapter topics and with the related projects or artifacts. The comprehensive matrix aligning CEC professional standards, Praxis Standards, and INTASC principles is available in the appendix of the textbook.

CEC Standards	Chapter Topics	Related Projects or Artifacts
1	<ul><li>Disproportionate representation.</li><li>Zero reject.</li><li>Expulsion and discipline.</li><li>Procedural due process.</li><li>Long-term results of special education.</li><li>Socioeconomic characteristics.</li><li>Family education level.</li><li>Racial and ethnic trends.</li><li>Appropriate education.</li></ul>	Focus on Curriculum and Instructional Choices, Focus on Technology, Focus on Collaboration, Focus on Diversity.
2	<ul><li>Long-term results of special education.</li></ul>	Focus on Diversity
3	<ul><li>Instructional needs of students with disabilities.</li><li>Who are students with disabilities?</li><li>Long-term results of special education.</li><li>Family education level.</li><li>Racial and ethnic trends.</li><li>Appropriate education.</li></ul>	Focus on Curriculum and Instructional Choices, Focus on Technology, Focus on Collaboration
4	<ul><li>Who are students with disabilities?</li><li>Instructional needs of students with disabilities.</li></ul>	Focus on Collaboration, Focus on Curriculum and Instructional Choices
5	<ul><li>Who are students with disabilities?</li><li>Instructional needs of students with disabilities.</li><li>Expulsion and discipline.</li><li>Parent-Student Participation.</li></ul>	Focus on Curriculum and Instructional Choices, Focus on Technology, Focus on Collaboration
6	<ul><li>Parent-Student Participation.</li></ul>	Focus on Collaboration
7	<ul><li>Who are students with disabilities?</li><li>Instructional needs of students with disabilities.</li></ul>	Focus on Curriculum and Instructional Choices, Focus on Diversity.
8	<ul><li>Who are students with disabilities?</li><li>Instructional needs of students with disabilities.</li><li>Nondiscriminatory evaluation.</li><li>Appropriate education.</li></ul>	Focus on Curriculum and Instructional Choices, Focus on Technology, Focus on Collaboration, Focus on Diversity.

(continued – Standards/Topics – Project Alignment Matrix)

	Chapter Topics	Related Projects or Artifacts
9	• Disproportionate representation. • Special Education personnel. • Zero reject. • Expulsion and discipline. • Overlapping services to support students with disabilities. • Procedural due process. • Long-term results of special education. • Family education level. • Racial and ethnic trends. • Appropriate education.	Focus on Curriculum and Instructional Choices, Focus on Technology, Focus on Collaboration, Focus on Diversity.
10	• Special Education personnel. • Parent-Student Participation. • Overlapping services to support students with disabilities.	Focus on Collaboration, Focus on Technology
Praxis Standards	**Chapter Topics**	**Related Projects or Artifacts**
1	• Who are students with disabilities? • Instructional needs of students with disabilities. • Disproportionate representation.	Focus on Curriculum and Instructional Choices
2	• Discrimination. • Judicial decisions. • Individuals with Disabilities Education Act. • Principles of IDEA. • Rehabilitation services. • Section 504 and the ADA.	Focus on Technology, Focus on Collaboration
3	• Special education personnel. • Least restrictive environment. • Free appropriate public education.	Focus on Curriculum and Instructional Choices, Focus on Collaboration
INTASC Principles	**Chapter Topics**	**Related Projects or Artifacts**
1	• Who are students with disabilities? • Instructional needs of students with disabilities. • Disproportionate representation. • Special Education personnel.	Focus on Curriculum and Instructional Choices, Focus on Technology, Focus on Collaboration
2	• Who are students with disabilities? • Instructional needs of students with disabilities.	Focus on Curriculum and Instructional Choices, Focus on Technology
3	• Instructional needs of students with disabilities.	Focus on Curriculum and Instructional Choices
4	• Instructional needs of students with disabilities.	
5	• Instructional needs of students with disabilities.	

(continued – Standards/Topics – Project Alignment Matrix)

7	• Instructional needs of students with disabilities. • Characteristics of students with disabilities.	Focus on Curriculum and Instructional Choices
8	• Nondiscriminatory evaluation. • Appropriate education.	Focus on Diversity
9	• Special Education personnel.	Focus on Collaboration
10	• Parent-Student Participation. • Overlapping services to support students with disabilities.	Focus on Curriculum and Instructional Choices, Focus on Collaboration

Materials Available on the Companion Website

Self-quizzes on chapter content

Lists of available videos and class activities

Sample IEP, IFSP, and ITP

Community Map

Links to related websites and resources

Links to sample projects or artifacts

Link to "Expanding the Circle" activity focusing on collaboration

Other case study related materials to support comprehensive understanding

Graphic Organizer for Chapter 1

Chapter 2
ENSURING PROGRESS IN THE GENERAL CURRICULUM:
UNIVERSAL DESIGN AND INCLUSION

Chapter Overview

To understand the benefits of using a universally designed curriculum, universally designed instruction, or universally designed evaluation, it is important to understand how these approaches to teaching and learning support students with exceptionalities in progressing with the general education curriculum. In this chapter you will learn important background information on standards-based reform and recent accountability measures that are changing the way we structure our classrooms. In addition, you will be presented with an overview of placement options that interact with these accountability measures, as well as background information on the inclusion of students with exceptionalities in the general education classroom. While this chapter goes into some detail on the Individuals with Disabilities Education Act, the emphasis is on the implementation of the legislation's key principles.

 Don't forget to access the video and audio vignettes that accompany this chapter...

Instructional Goals

After reading this chapter you will be able to:
1. Understand how students with disabilities interact within systems of accountability.
2. Reflect on how the use of a universally designed learning experience can support students with exceptionalities and contribute to the overall quality of curriculum and instruction.
3. Differentiate among various placement options for students with disabilities.
4. Recall the key characteristics of inclusion.
5. Understand why progressing through the general education curriculum is important for students with exceptionalities.

Guiding Questions

Don't forget about the Graphic Organizer available on the Companion Website.

What does it mean to progress in the general curriculum?

What is standards-based reform?

What is No Child Left Behind and how does it relate to special education?

What are content standards?

What are performance standards?

What types of assessment accommodations are acceptable?

What is high-stakes accountability?

How did the concept of Universal Design for Learning begin?

How do you augment or alter curriculum, instruction, and evaluation?

What are current placement trends for providing support for students with disabilities?

What are key characteristics of inclusion?

What do the student outcomes associated with inclusion include?

Key Terms

In the space provided below, define the key terms in the chapter.

No Child Left Behind

General Curriculum

High-stakes Accountability

Inclusion

Individuals with Disabilities Education Act

Augment

Curriculum

Instruction

Universal Design

Case Study Summary and Focus Activity

Case Study Summary

Heather and Star Morgan, students at Luff Elementary School, have been identified as having mild mental retardation and multiple disabilities. Heather, a third grader, loves reading and is in a school where expectations for her are held high. Star, Heather's younger sister, is in first grade. Like Heather, the expectation that Star be an involved member of the classroom community is high. Star uses sign language to read aloud with classmates and participates in the general education classroom at a high level. Heather is paving the way for her younger sister in many ways, including providing the faculty of Luff an opportunity to understand what accommodations are necessary on state assessments for students with exceptionalities. Heather and Star are fortunate to attend a school committed to providing a learning experience that promotes successful independence. Heather utilizes special technologies and support systems to show her progress through the general education curriculum. By using a computer to compose her writing and answering multiplication questions verbally, Heather is able to demonstrate what she knows and is not hindered in doing so by her disability. Accordingly, Heather is able to use these practiced accommodations during state assessments.

Focus Activity

Collaboration Connection...	Your Thoughts...
What are some of your concerns about involving students with disabilities in high-stakes accountability systems?	

Diversity Link...	Your Thoughts...
How can you as a teacher safeguard against overrepresentation of certain populations of students?	

Focus on Inclusion...	Your Thoughts...
Why is it important to understand the different placement options for students with exceptionalities?	
How can you, as a professional working with students with exceptionalities, promote inclusion in the classroom or school?	
What is your perspective on inclusion?	

Universal Design Application...	Your Thoughts...
In what ways do you feel you are prepared or unprepared to use the concepts of Universal Design for Learning?	
What is your response to the expectation that students with exceptionalities progress through the general education curriculum?	

Artifact or Project Opportunities

Focus on Curriculum and Instructional Choices:

Read the article, "Getting the 'Big Picture' of IEP Goals and State Standards," by James Walsh, published in the Council for Exceptional Children's journal *Teaching Exceptional Children*, Volume 33, Number 5. The article is available online at http://journals.cec.sped.org (a direct hyperlink to the article is available on the Companion Website). After reading the article, write a brief reflection connecting the author's statements, the information provided in Chapter 2, and your opinions on how standards are connected with the teaching and learning of students with exceptionalities.

Focus on Technology:

Visit the Center for Applied Special Technologies website at www.cast.org (a hyperlink is also available on the Companion Website). After visiting the CAST website, review a sample of the materials on Universal Design for Learning. Upon completion of your review, create a brief summary of at least one article, answering the question, "How can I utilize the concepts of Universal Design for Learning as a teacher?"

Focus on Collaboration:

Compose a brief position statement answering the question, "How do you feel collaboration among educational professionals can support a student in progressing through the general education curriculum?"

Focus on Diversity:

In the chapter, the authors present six placement categories. Imagine that you are working with a student who is placed in special education outside the regular class more than 60 percent of the day. In the context of the grade level or area of education in which you intend to work, describe three ways you could provide additional peer-interaction for that student given your expected daily schedule.

Spot Check

1. What key changes were observed in how teachers plan and facilitate instruction after the implementation of standards-based curriculum?

2. What are the differences between content and performance standards?

3. What is high-stakes accountability?

4. List the benefits of simultaneously implementing a universally designed curriculum, instruction, and evaluation.

5. What is inclusion?

6. What does it mean to "progress through the general education curriculum"?

7. What are the most frequent responses of parents with regard to inclusion?

Questions and Reflections
(After reading the chapter, use this area to keep track of your questions or reflections.)

#Standards/Topics – Project Alignment Matrix

The following professional standards are addressed in Chapter 2 within the correlating chapter topics and with the related projects or artifacts. A comprehensive matrix aligning CEC professional standards, Praxis Standards, and INTASC principles is available in the appendix of the textbook.

CEC Standards	Chapter Topics	Related Projects or Artifacts
1	• Standards-based reform. • Accountability issues. • Inclusion.	Focus on Curriculum and Instruction, Focus on Technology, Focus on Collaboration, Focus on Diversity
2	• Universally designed curriculum, instruction, and evaluation. • Restructuring teaching and learning.	Focus on Technology, Focus on Curriculum and Instruction
3	• Progressing in the general curriculum. • Inclusion. • Restructuring teaching and learning. • Assessment accommodations.	Focus on Curriculum and Instruction, Focus on Technology, Focus on Collaboration, Focus on Diversity
4	• Progressing in the general curriculum. • Standards-based reform. • Universally designed curriculum, instruction, and evaluation.	Focus on Curriculum and Instruction, Focus on Technology, Focus on Collaboration, Focus on Diversity
5	• Progressing in the general curriculum. • Accountability issues. • Universally designed curriculum, instruction, and evaluation.	Focus on Collaboration, Focus on Curriculum and Instruction, Focus on Technology
6	• Parent responses to inclusion.	Focus on Collaboration.
7	• Progressing in the general curriculum. • Universally designed curriculum, instruction, and evaluation. • Restructuring teaching and learning.	Focus on Curriculum and Instruction, Focus on Technology, Focus on Collaboration, Focus on Diversity
8	• Progressing in the general curriculum. • Standards-based reform. • Assessment accommodations. • Accountability issues. • Universally designed curriculum, instruction, and evaluation.	Focus on Curriculum and Instruction, Focus on Technology, Focus on Collaboration, Focus on Diversity
9	• Standards-based reform. • Accountability issues. • Inclusion. • Parent responses to inclusion.	Focus on Curriculum and Instruction, Focus on Technology, Focus on Diversity
10	• Parent responses to inclusion.	Focus on Collaboration

(continued – Standards/Topics – Project Alignment Matrix)

Praxis Standards	Chapter Topics	Related Projects or Artifacts
1	• Progressing in the general curriculum. • Characteristics of inclusion.	Focus on Technology, Focus on Collaboration, Focus on Diversity
2	• Standards-based reform. • Accountability issues.	Focus on Curriculum and Instruction
3	• Universally designed curriculum, instruction, and evaluation.	Focus on Diversity

INTASC Principles	Chapter Topics	Related Projects or Artifacts
1	• Universally designed curriculum, instruction, and evaluation.	Focus on Technology, Focus on Diversity
3	• Universally designed curriculum, instruction, and evaluation.	Focus on Technology, Focus on Diversity
4	• Universally designed curriculum, instruction, and evaluation.	Focus on Technology, Focus on Diversity
7	• Accountability issues. • Assessment accommodations. • Progressing in the general curriculum.	Focus on Technology, Focus on Curriculum and Instruction
8	• Accountability issues. • Assessment accommodations. • Progressing in the general curriculum. • Universally designed curriculum, instruction, and evaluation.	Focus on Curriculum and Instruction, Focus on Technology, Focus on Collaboration, Focus on Diversity
10	• Characteristics of inclusion.	Focus on Collaboration, Focus on Diversity

Materials Available on the Companion Website

Self-quizzes on chapter content

Lists of available videos and class activities

Links to related websites and resources

Links to sample projects or artifacts

Link to the article "Getting the "Big Picture" of IEP Goals and State Standards"

Other case study related materials to support comprehensive understanding

Assessment and accommodations planning guide

Graphic Organizer for Chapter 2

Chapter 3
ENSURING PROGRESS IN THE GENERAL CURRICULUM:
COLLABORATION AND MULTICULTURAL RESPONSIVENESS

Chapter Overview

Understanding how collaboration and inclusion are intertwined is critical to ensuring the success of students with disabilities in the general education curriculum. This chapter presents information on how collaboration takes place in the classroom and school context, and provides important information on how collaboration can be fostered with multiple stakeholders. In addition, the authors present related information on multicultural awareness and the effects of culture on collaboration. It is important that you understand that collaborative and inclusive practices enhance successful progression through the general curriculum for students with disabilities.

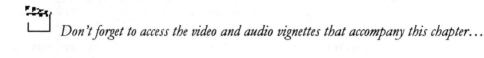 *Don't forget to access the video and audio vignettes that accompany this chapter…*

Instructional Goals

After reading this chapter you will be able to:
1. Describe how collaboration can enable students with disabilities to progress in the general curriculum.
2. Discuss the various stakeholders in collaboration.
3. Identify effective approaches to collaboration.
4. Describe the process involved in creating collaborative teams.
5. Connect multicultural responsiveness with student success in the general curriculum.
6. Describe how culture can influence roles and expectations in collaborative teams.

Guiding Questions

Don't forget about the Graphic Organizer available on the Companion Website.

Who are the stakeholders in collaborative teams?

How can teachers or other professionals exert expert power?

What type of roles do related service providers fill?

How can an administrator's belief system and attention to inclusion affect the success of students with disabilities in inclusive settings?

What are the necessary elements of collaborative teams?

What is multicultural responsiveness?

How can cultural reciprocity influence collaboration?

How can multicultural responsiveness support the successful inclusion of students with disabilities?

Key Terms

In the space provided below, define the key terms in the chapter.

Inclusion

Collaboration

Multicultural Responsiveness

Mediation

Related Service Providers

Overrepresentation

Case Study and Focus Activity

Case Study Summary

The stories of Ronda, Donald, and Luisa are unfortunately not uncommon. Ronda, experiencing delays in being initially evaluated for special education and then provided with less than adequate support services, is now identified as having "other health impairments" under the Individuals with Disabilities Education Act (IDEA). Her family recruited the assistance of the Pyramid Parent Training Center in order to simply initiate a re-evaluation, and has finally been provided an opportunity to see their daughter progress academically and socially. Donald, who has been identified as having autism, encountered a frustrating educational experience when his teachers and other service providers felt unprepared to meet his needs. After he enlisted the assistance of the Pyramid Parent Training Center like Ronda, the school began to use the technique known as positive behavioral support to improve learning and teaching for Donald. Luckily, Donald is now experiencing some successes at school. Luisa, another student introduced in the case study, has not yet been provided access to a successful educational experience. With financial struggles and other frustrations facing her family, Luisa's parents went to another community center for assistance. This time the Catholic Charities stepped in to help. Providing supports to help the family become more satisfied with their quality of life, they are gradually working toward understanding Luisa's struggles at school.

Focus Activity

Collaboration Connection...	Your Thoughts...
What are your concerns related to being a member of a collaborative team?	

(continued – Collaboration Connection ...)

How well prepared are you for working with a collaborative team?	
How do you think the role you take during group work or other group-related activities foreshadows the role you might take on collaborative teams?	

Diversity Link...	Your Thoughts...
How have each of the students in the case study summary been affected by their family background, community location, and access to support?	

Focus on Inclusion...	Your Thoughts...
How can students be included but not supported?	
How have Ronda, Donald, and Luisa been included?	

Universal Design Application...	Your Thoughts...
How have the experiences of Ronda, Donald, and Luisa been culturally responsive?	
How would the experiences of Ronda, Donald, and Luisa have been different if an effort had been made with regard to cultural responsiveness?	

✐ Artifact or Project Opportunities

Focus on Curriculum and Instructional Choices:
Identify the educational needs of each student presented in the case study. After identifying those needs, compose a brief summary of ways in which those needs could be met in the classroom context.

Focus on Technology:
On the Power of 2 website (www.powerof2.org), visit the online training section of the site (www.powerof2.org/modules). Create an account (free of charge) and enter the Co-Teaching module. Access the Case Studies option, review the first case study about Ben and Letitia, and complete the activities. The results of your work can be printed

or saved in a portfolio within your personal Power of 2 account. This activity offers you an example of online professional development, and provides access to an excellent resource.

Focus on Diversity:
Thinking about the case studies (Ronda, Donald, and Luisa) that were presented in the chapter, choose one student and compose a brief position paper citing your thoughts, opinions, and concerns about the information that was shared. Include how, as an educational professional, you will respond to similar situations.

Spot Check

1. What is co-teaching?

2. How can culture influence collaboration?

3. In what ways do administrators affect collaboration in schools?

4. What are appropriate roles for paraprofessionals?

5. How can students benefit from collaboration?

Questions and Reflections
(After reading the chapter, use this area to keep track of your questions or reflections.)

#Standards/Topics – Project Alignment Matrix

The following professional standards are addressed in Chapter 3 within the correlating chapter topics and with the related projects or artifacts. A comprehensive matrix aligning CEC professional standards, Praxis Standards, and INTASC principles is available in the appendix of the textbook.

CEC Standards	Chapter Topics	Related Projects or Artifacts
3	• Progressing in the general curriculum. • Multicultural responsiveness.	Focus on Diversity, Focus on Curriculum and Instruction
4	• Progressing in the general curriculum.	Focus on Curriculum and Instruction
5	• Progressing in the general curriculum.	Focus on Curriculum and Instruction
7	• Progressing in the general curriculum.	Focus on Curriculum and Instruction
8	• Progressing in the general curriculum.	Focus on Curriculum and Instruction
9	• Multicultural responsiveness.	Focus on Diversity
10	• Collaboration to support student needs.	Focus on Technology
Praxis Standards	**Chapter Topics**	**Related Projects or Artifacts**
1	• Progressing in the general curriculum. • Multicultural responsiveness.	Focus on Diversity, Focus on Curriculum and Instruction
3	• Collaboration to support student needs. • Related service providers.	Focus on Curriculum and Instruction, Focus on Technology
INTASC Principles	**Chapter Topics**	**Related Projects or Artifacts**
1	• Progressing in the general curriculum. • Multicultural responsiveness.	Focus on Diversity, Focus on Curriculum and Instruction
2	• Multicultural responsiveness.	Focus on Curriculum and Instruction
3	• Progressing in the general curriculum. • Multicultural responsiveness.	Focus on Diversity, Focus on Curriculum and Instruction, Focus on Technology
5	• Multicultural responsiveness.	Focus on Curriculum and Instruction
7	• Collaboration to support student needs. • Related service providers.	Focus on Curriculum and Instruction, Focus on Technology
10	• Multicultural responsiveness.	Focus on Diversity

Materials Available on the Companion Website

Self-quizzes on chapter content
Links to related websites and resources
Links to sample projects or artifacts
Link to the Power of 2 website
Other case study related materials to support comprehensive understanding
Graphic Organizer for Chapter 3

Chapter 4
LEARNING DISABILITIES

Chapter Overview

The presence of a specific learning disability is not uncommon in most of today's classrooms. In fact, learning disabilities account for more than half of the students being served nationally under the Individuals with Disabilities Education Act. Since learning disabilities are the most commonly observed disability in the classrooms of the 21st century, it is important that classroom teachers be able to recognize their characteristics. But it doesn't stop there. Understanding what interventions or augmentations are possible is key to making meaningful instructional and curriculum choices for students in the classroom. This chapter will introduce you to learning disabilities, their common characteristics and causes, collaborative approaches that compliment efforts in the classroom, and instructional approaches to increase the success of a students with learning disabilities in the general curriculum.

 Don't forget to access the video and audio vignettes that accompany this chapter…

Instructional Goals

After reading this chapter you will be able to:
1. Describe the characteristics of a learning disability.
2. Discuss and understand the basic components of a universally designed curriculum.
3. Recognize the importance of student progress with the general curriculum.
4. Understand the benefits of collaboration and communication across settings.
5. Connect knowledge to specific case studies.
6. Create lesson plans that augment instructional and curriculum choices to insure the success of students with learning disabilities in the classroom.

Guiding Questions

Don't forget about the Graphic Organizer available on the Companion Website.

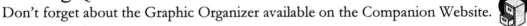

How do we identify students with learning disabilities?

What are the characteristics of a learning disability?

What is Dyslexia?

What is Dysgraphia?

What content area is Dyscalculia associated with?

How is memory affected by a specific learning disability?

How can a student's interpersonal skills be affected by a specific learning disability?

How can a student's self-concept be influenced by a learning disability?

What are the causes of learning disabilities?

How prevalent are learning disabilities in today's classrooms?

What is curriculum-based assessment?

How can the universally designed curriculum interact with the support provided to students with learning disabilities?

Why is collaboration an essential component to working with students with learning disabilities?

Key Terms

In the space provided below, define the key terms in the chapter.

Curriculum-based assessment

Dysgraphia

Dyslexia

Metacognition

Processessing

Case Study and Focus Activity

Case Study Summary

Tony Lavender is a sixth-grade student who happens to have a learning disability. His work ethic and ambition have helped him along the way; however, he has had to overcome past failures and the fears that those have instilled. Tony has made progressive strides during the past few years, considering how little interaction he has had with the special education teacher during his first year of middle school. Though it is now clear that he has the ability to fully participate in the general education classroom, during the next few years it will become critical that he develop appropriate social skills.

Focus Activity

Collaboration Connection...	Your Thoughts...
How has collaboration supported Tony?	
How can special and general educators work together to support Tony in the general education curriculum?	
Diversity Link...	**Your Thoughts...**
How can Tony's social skills be developed?	

How has Tony been included in the general education classroom?	

Focus on Inclusion...	Your Thoughts...
How are students with specific learning disabilities included in the general education curriculum?	
How likely is it that a student with a specific learning disability will be included in the general education classroom?	

Universal Design Application...	Your Thoughts...
How can the curriculum and instructional choices of the teacher influence Tony's success?	
How can Tony's strengths be used to ensure his success in the general curriculum?	

Artifact or Project Opportunities

Focus on Curriculum and Instructional Choices:
Using a lesson plan that you have created or a model lesson plan found on the Companion Website, identify ways in which you could incorporate Tony's strengths to create a more inclusive class-wide presentation of materials.

Focus on Technology:
With the same lesson plan, simply list five ways you could incorporate technology to better facilitate the lesson. In addition, find at least two Internet resources that could be used to complement the instructional learning goals of the lesson plan.

Focus on Collaboration:
Again, using the lesson plan that you have modified, list persons in the school or greater community that could support you as a classroom teacher during instruction, or support students during independent learning/working time.

🔮 Spot Check

1. List the possible characteristics of a student with a learning disability.

2. Describe the basic tenets of a universally designed curriculum.

3. Identify three ways in which collaboration can affect the success of a student with a learning disability in your classroom.

4. When would a teacher use a learning strategy in the classroom?

Questions and Reflections
(After reading the chapter, use this area to keep track of your questions or reflections.)

⌗Standards/Topics – Project Alignment Matrix

The following professional standards are addressed in Chapter 4 within the correlating chapter topics and with the related projects or artifacts. The comprehensive matrix aligning CEC professional standards, Praxis Standards, and INTASC principles is available in the appendix of the textbook.

CEC Standards	Chapter Topics	Related Projects or Artifacts
1	• Characteristics of learning disabilities. • Characteristics of specific learning disabilities as they relate to certain areas, as well as behavioral, social, and emotional characteristics. • Augmenting curriculum and instruction.	Focus on Curriculum and Instruction, Focus on Collaboration, Focus on Technology
2	• Characteristics of specific learning disabilities as they relate to certain areas, as well as behavioral, social, and emotional characteristics. • Characteristics of learning disabilities.	Focus on Curriculum and Instruction, Focus on Collaboration
3	• Curricular and instructional needs of students with learning disabilities. • Augmenting curriculum and instruction. • Collaborative relationships. • Characteristics of learning disabilities. • Specific instructional choices for students with learning disabilities. • Characteristics of specific learning disabilities as they relate to certain areas, as well as behavioral, social, and emotional characteristics. • Identification of developmentally appropriate social goals.	Focus on Curriculum and Instruction, Focus on Technology, Focus on Collaboration
4	• Specific instructional choices for students with learning disabilities. • Characteristics of specific learning disabilities as they relate to certain areas, as well as behavioral, social, and emotional characteristics.	Focus on Curriculum and Instruction, Focus on Collaboration
5	• Collaborative relationships. • Characteristics of learning disabilities. • Characteristics of specific learning disabilities as they relate to certain areas, as well as behavioral, social, and emotional characteristics. • Identification of developmentally appropriate social goals.	Focus on Curriculum and Instruction, Focus on Collaboration, Focus on Technology

(continued – Standards/Topics – Project Alignment Matrix)

7	• Collaborative relationships. • Specific instructional choices for students with learning disabilities. • Augmenting curriculum and instruction.	Focus on Curriculum and Instruction, Focus on Collaboration, Focus on Technology
10	• Collaborative relationships.	

Praxis Standards	Chapter Topics	Related Projects or Artifacts
1	• Characteristics of specific learning disabilities as they relate to certain areas, as well as behavioral, social, and emotional characteristics. • Identification of developmentally appropriate social goals. • Relevant resources and materials that contribute to the literature base on instructional strategies.	Focus on Curriculum and Instruction
3	• Collaborative relationships. • Collaboration to support instruction. • Specific instructional choices for students with learning disabilities.	Focus on Curriculum and Instruction

INTASC Principles	Chapter Topics	Related Projects or Artifacts
1	• Identification of developmentally appropriate social goals.	Focus on Curriculum and Instruction, Focus on Collaboration, Focus on Technology
2	• Characteristics of specific learning disabilities as they relate to certain areas, as well as behavioral, social, and emotional characteristics.	Focus on Curriculum and Instruction, Focus on Technology
3	• Characteristics of specific learning disabilities as they relate to certain areas, as well as behavioral, social, and emotional characteristics. • Augmenting curriculum and instruction. • Relevant resources and materials that contribute to the literature base on instructional strategies.	Focus on Curriculum and Instruction, Focus on Collaboration, Focus on Technology
4	• Relevant resources and materials that contribute to the literature base on instructional strategies.	Focus on Curriculum and Instruction, Focus on Technology
5	• Characteristics of specific learning disabilities as they relate to certain areas, as well as behavioral, social, and emotional characteristics. • Identification of developmentally appropriate social goals.	Focus on Curriculum and Instruction, Focus on Technology
6	• Specific instructional choices for students with learning disabilities.	Focus on Technology

(continued – Standards/Topics – Project Alignment Matrix)

7	• Specific instructional choices for students with learning disabilities.	Focus on Curriculum and Instruction
10	• Collaborative relationships.	Focus on Collaboration

Materials Available on the Companion Website

Self-quizzes on chapter content

Lists of available videos and class activities

Sample lesson plans

Cooperative learning activity

Links to related websites and resources

Links to sample projects or artifacts

Other case study related materials to support comprehensive understanding

Graphic Organizer for Chapter 4

Chapter 5
EMOTIONAL OR BEHAVIORAL DISORDERS

Chapter Overview

Emotional or behavioral disorders are complex and varied. This chapter presents information that may clarify the definitions and characteristics of emotional or behavioral disorders. In addition, the authors present evaluation procedures and meaningful ways to include students in the classroom setting. In order to meet the needs of students with emotional or behavioral disorders, it is important that educational professionals understand how curricular and instructional approaches can be augmented to set each student up for success.

 Don't forget to access the video and audio vignettes that accompany this chapter...

Instructional Goals

After reading this chapter you will be able to:
1. Describe the characteristics of emotional or behavioral disorders.
2. Understand the differences between biological and environmental influences.
3. Utilize basic approaches to effectively adapt assessments for students with emotional or behavioral disorders.
4. Understand the importance of collaboration in working with students with emotional or behavioral disorders.

Guiding Questions

Don't forget about the Graphic Organizer available on the Companion Website.

How do you define emotional or behavioral disorders?

What is social maladjustment?

What are the characteristics of emotional or behavioral disorders?

What is an anxiety disorder?

What is a mood disorder?

What is a bipolar disorder?

What is oppositional defiant disorder?

How would you describe a conduct disorder?

What is schizophrenia?

What would an example of an externalized behavior be?
How do students internalize behavior?

What are the biological causes of emotional or behavioral disorders?

What environmental stressors are related to emotional or behavioral disorders?

Key Terms

In the space provided below, define the key terms in the chapter.

Anxiety disorder

Bipolar disorder

Depression

Eating disorder

Heterogeneous

Post-traumatic stress disorder

Social maladjustment

Case Study and Focus Activity

Case Study Summary

Matt Ackinclose, a 14-year-old in the eighth grade, once took over 20 prescription pills a day to manage his behavior. However, now he relies on his own resiliency and takes only two medications during the course of his day. With the persistence of his mother and supports from various other stakeholders like his social worker, Rebecca, Matt has made progress in both social and academic skills. By focusing on Matt's strengths, interests, and moments of positive and appropriate behaviors, Rebecca created opportunities for Matt to work with Charlotte Hott, a special education teacher. Charlotte entered into a partnership with Matt, simultaneously providing him the cooperative relationship he needed and helping him to navigate simple changes in expectations that could help Matt be successful.

Focus Activity

Collaboration Connection...	Your Thoughts...
How has collaboration supported Matt?	
How has Rebecca contributed to Matt and Charlotte's partnership?	
Diversity Link...	Your Thoughts...
How did Charlotte's openness contribute to	

Matt's success?	

Focus on Inclusion...	Your Thoughts...
What concerns would be raised by including students like Matt in the general education classroom?	
Why was Charlotte's response to Matt's needs so unique?	

Universal Design Application...	Your Thoughts...
How can Matt and Charlotte's positive partnership support Matt's learning goals?	

Artifact or Project Opportunities

Focus on Curriculum and Instructional Choices:
Read the article "Learning to Cooperate: A Teacher's Perspective," by Charlotte Sonnier-York and Pokey Stanford, published in the Council for Exceptional Children's journal *Teaching Exceptional Children*, Volume 34, Number 6. The article is available online at http://journals.cec.sped.org (a direct hyperlink to the article is available on the Companion Website). After reading the article, write a brief description of how cooperative learning can be used in their classroom and what social skills could be embedded into those activities.

Focus on Collaboration:
Prepare a personal mission statement that focuses on your approach to teaching and working with others (including students). Be honest and open in your presentation of your values, beliefs, and goals as an educational professional.

Spot Check

1. How are students with social maladjustment served under IDEA?

2. How are students with emotional or behavioral disorders heterogeneous?

3. What changes can students suffering from depression experience?

4. What is oppositional defiant disorder?

5. Why are students with internalizing behaviors less likely to receive services for emotional or behavioral disorders?

Questions and Reflections

(After reading the chapter, use this area to keep track of your questions or reflections.)

#Standards/Topics – Project Alignment Matrix

The following professional standards are addressed in Chapter 5 within the correlating chapter topics and with the related projects or artifacts. The comprehensive matrix aligning CEC professional standards, Praxis Standards, and INTASC principles is available in the appendix of the textbook.

CEC Standards	Chapter Topics	Related Projects or Artifacts
1	• Characteristics of emotional or behavioral disorders. • Adapting instruction and assessment. • Environmental stressors. • Nature and extent of services. • Understanding causes.	Focus on Curriculum and Instruction
2	• Internalizing and externalizing behaviors. • Characteristics of emotional or behavioral disorders. • Nature and extent of services. • Developing resilience.	
3	• Characteristics of emotional or behavioral disorders. • Internalizing and externalizing behaviors.	
4	• Adapting instruction and assessment.	Focus on Collaboration
5	• Developing resilience. • Collaborative relationships. • Internalizing and externalizing behaviors. • Environmental stressors.	
7	• Adapting instruction and assessment.	Focus on Curricular and Instructional Choices
8	• Adapting instruction and assessment.	Focus on Curricular and Instructional Choices
9	• Environmental stressors. • Nature and extent of services. • Developing resilience. • Understanding causes.	
10	• Collaborative relationships.	Focus on Collaboration

(continued – Standards/Topics – Project Alignment Matrix)

Praxis Standards	Chapter Topics	Related Projects or Artifacts
1	• Characteristics of emotional or behavioral disorders. • Internalizing and externalizing behaviors. • Understanding causes.	Focus on Curriculum and Instruction
2	• Manifestation determination.	Focus on Collaboration
3	• Collaboration. • Utilizing universal design for learning. • Cognitive and academic characteristics.	Focus on Collaboration, Focus on Curriculum and Instruction

INTASC Principles	Chapter Topics	Related Projects or Artifacts
1	• Characteristics of emotional or behavior disorders. • Adapting instruction and assessment.	Focus on Curriculum and Instruction
2	• Characteristics of emotional or behavioral disorders. • Adapting instruction and assessment. • Cognitive and academic characteristics.	Focus on Curriculum and Instruction
3	• Characteristics of emotional or behavioral disorders. • Internalizing and externalizing behaviors. • Understanding causes.	Focus on Curriculum and Instruction
4	• Characteristics of emotional or behavioral disorders. • Adapting instruction and assessment. • Cognitive and academic characteristics.	Focus on Curriculum and Instruction
5	• Characteristics of emotional or behavioral disorders. • Adapting instruction and assessment.	Focus on Collaboration, Focus on Curriculum and Instruction
7	• Collaboration. • Utilizing universal design for learning. • Cognitive and academic characteristics.	Focus on Collaboration, Focus on Curriculum and Instruction
8	• Adapting instruction and assessment.	Focus on Collaboration, Focus on Curriculum and Instruction
10	• Collaboration.	Focus on Collaboration

Materials Available on the Companion Website

Self-quizzes on chapter content
Lists of available videos and class activities
Links to related websites and resources
Links to sample projects or artifacts
Link to the article "Learning to Cooperate: A Teacher's Perspective"
Other case study related materials to support comprehensive understanding
Graphic Organizer for Chapter 5

Chapter 6
ATTENTION-DEFICIT/HYPERACTIVITY DISORDER

Chapter Overview

It is easy, given the attention ADD and AD/HD receive in the media, to make assumptions about what it means to be identified as having one of these debilitating conditions. However, it is important that as educational professionals, students understand how AD/HD can influence a student in the classroom setting. Information on the placement of AD/HD within the context of IDEA lays the foundation for understanding how educational, social, and behavioral interventions can be implemented effectively in the classroom. This chapter presents characteristics and definitions, but also provides important information on teaching, including, and collaborating to meet student needs.

 Don't forget to access the video and audio vignettes that accompany this chapter...

Instructional Goals

After reading this chapter you will be able to:
1. Identify causes of AD/HD.
2. Understand the complexities of AD/HD in relation to providing services for students under IDEA.
3. Recall the subtypes of AD/HD provided by the American Psychiatric Association.
4. Describe positive traits associated with AD/HD.
5. Understand the social, emotional, and behavioral needs of students with AD/HD.
6. Describe how curricular and instructional choices can be augmented to meet the needs of students with AD/HD.

Guiding Questions

Don't forget about the Graphic Organizer available on the Companion Website.

How do you recognize AD/HD?

How is AD/HD attended to in IDEA?

What does it mean to be predominately inattentive?

What are the three "types" of AD/HD?

How do students internalize speech?

What are positive traits of AD/HD?

How can the environment connect with explaining AD/HD?

How does genetics connect with AD/HD?

How can curriculum be altered to meet the needs of students with AD/HD?

Key Terms

In the space provided below, define the key terms in the chapter.

Combined type

Hyperactivity

Multimodal

Novelty

Variety

Self-efficacy

Case Study and Focus Activity

Case Study Summary

Kelsey Blankenship is a fourth-grade student who has AD/HD. Kelsey has struggled in the past with appropriate classroom behavior, social skills, and attention to homework or other school-related tasks. She is lucky, though, to have an outstanding support system in her grandparents, teacher, and therapists. While Kelsey challenged the patience of her primary caregivers (it always seemed to be a struggle to gain her cooperation), she has made strides in taking responsibility and putting her best effort forward. Many of her successes have been tied to the team of people that support her; their collaboration and supportive communication have provided a foundation for Kelsey to grow and learn.

Focus Activity

Collaboration Connection...	Your Thoughts...
How has collaboration supported Kelsey?	
How has Kelsey's team helped to alleviate some of the stress of her primary caregivers?	

Diversity Link...	Your Thoughts...
In what ways has Kelsey's team supported her involvement in activities that build upon her strengths?	

Focus on Inclusion...	Your Thoughts...
How could Kelsey's team communicate more effectively about what is working and what is not working to support her?	

Universal Design Application...	Your Thoughts...
How have Kelsey's strengths been used to support her in specific learning goals?	

Artifact or Project Opportunities

Focus on Curriculum and Instructional Choices:
Using a sample lesson plan (found on the Companion Website or in other resources), identify ways in which the lesson could be adapted to add variety, choice, or activity. Describe how those adaptations create a lesson better suited to meet the needs of individuals with AD/HD.

Focus on Collaboration:
Read the article "We Need to Talk: Communication Strategies for Effective Collaboration," by Heidi Hollingsworth, published in the Council for Exceptional Children's journal *Teaching Exceptional Children*, Volume 33, Number 5. The article is available online at http://journals.cec.sped.org (a direct hyperlink to the article is available on the Companion Website). After reading the article, write a brief reflection focusing on how Kelsey's "team of supports" could improve or alter their communication.

Focus on Diversity:
In Kelsey's case study, one of her teachers mentioned how other students responded to Kelsey's behavior. Design and construct a bulletin board (either in full or in part by using a word processing or other computer program) that will teach or display social skills, expectations, or ways to respond to other people's behavior. Write a short description of the bulletin board and how you would use it in the classroom or other educational setting.

Spot Check

1. Is AD/HD considered a disability under IDEA?

2. What are the causes of AD/HD?

3. What are the strengths that can be associated with AD/HD?

4. What is a 504 Plan?

5. How can curriculum be augmented to meet the needs of students with AD/HD?

Questions and Reflections

(After reading the chapter, use this area to keep track of your questions or reflections.)

⌗Standards/Topics – Project Alignment Matrix

The following professional standards are addressed in Chapter 6 within the correlating chapter topics and with the related projects or artifacts. A comprehensive matrix aligning CEC professional standards, Praxis Standards, and INTASC principles is available in the appendix of the textbook.

CEC Standards	Chapter Topics	Related Projects or Artifacts
1	• Characteristics of AD/HD. • Three types of AD/HD. • Positive traits of individuals with AD/HD. • Determining nature and extent of services. • Evaluation procedures.	Focus on Curriculum and Instruction, Focus on Diversity
2	• Characteristics of AD/HD. • Three types of AD/HD. • Positive traits of individuals with AD/HD. • Determining nature and extent of services.	Focus on Diversity
3	• Characteristics of AD/HD. • Three types of AD/HD. • Positive traits of individuals with AD/HD. • Determining nature and extent of services.	Focus on Curriculum and Instruction, Focus on Diversity
5	• Positive traits of individuals with AD/HD. • Augmenting curriculum and instruction.	Focus on Curriculum and Instruction
6	• Communicating new developments.	Focus on Collaboration
7	• Augmenting curriculum and instruction. • Determining nature and extent of services.	Focus on Curriculum and Instruction, Focus on Diversity
8	• Evaluation procedures.	
9	• Evaluation procedures. • Communicating new developments.	Focus on Collaboration
10	• Collaboration. • Communicating new developments.	Focus on Collaboration

(continued – Standards/Topics – Project Alignment Matrix)

Praxis Standards	Chapter Topics	Related Projects or Artifacts
1	• Characteristics of AD/HD. • Three types of AD/HD.	Focus on Curriculum and Instruction
2	• Coverage of AD/HD under IDEA.	
3	• Collaboration. • Positive traits of individuals with AD/HD. • Augmenting curriculum and instruction.	Focus on Collaboration, Focus on Diversity

INTASC Principles	Chapter Topics	Related Projects or Artifacts
1	• Augmenting curriculum and instruction.	Focus on Curriculum and Instruction
2	• Augmenting curriculum and instruction.	Focus on Curriculum and Instruction
3	• Characteristics of AD/HD. • Three types of AD/HD. • Augmenting curriculum and instruction.	Focus on Curriculum and Instruction, Focus on Collaboration, Focus on Diversity
5	• Characteristics of AD/HD. • Positive traits of individuals with AD/HD. • Augmenting curriculum and instruction.	Focus on Curriculum and Instruction
10	• Collaboration.	Focus on Collaboration

Materials Available on the Companion Website

Self-quizzes on chapter content
Lists of available videos and class activities
Links to related websites and resources
Links to sample projects or artifacts
Link to the article "We Need to Talk: Communication Strategies for Effective Collaboration"
Sample lesson plan
Other case study related materials to support comprehensive understanding
Graphic Organizer for Chapter 6

Chapter 7
GIFTEDNESS

Chapter Overview

Gifted education is an important and oftentimes overlooked aspect of special education. In this chapter students will learn about the characteristics of gifted students and be provided examples of a wide variety of evaluation tools. It is essential that educational professionals understand the various components of giftedness and its relation to student success with the general education curriculum. In addition, being able to collaboratively implement appropriate curriculum and instruction is crucial to student success. Basic information and strategies for meeting student needs are presented.

 Don't forget to access the video and audio vignettes that accompany this chapter...

Instructional Goals

After reading this chapter you will be able to:
1. Understand the role of giftedness within special education.
2. Apply knowledge of Universal Design for Learning to the curriculum and instruction for gifted education.
3. Recall the behavioral and social characteristics of students identified as gifted or talented.
4. Reflect on the benefits of collaboration in supporting the education of students identified as gifted or talented.

Guiding Questions

Don't forget about the Graphic Organizer available on the Companion Website.

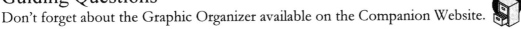

What are three factors associated with giftedness?

What is domain specific giftedness?

What is the theory of multiple intelligences?

What is emotional intelligence?

What are the characteristics of giftedness?

What are the social concerns of students who are identified as gifted or talented?

What is a creativity assessment?

What is the difference between product and performance assessment?

Key Terms

In the space provided below, define the key terms in the chapter.

Problem-based learning

Mentor

Type I enrichment

Type II enrichment

Type III enrichment

Case Study In-Class Activity

Case Study Summary

Briana is a middle school student who, over the course of her life, has been observed as being a gifted individual. Attending the Program for Exceptionally Gifted Students since third grade, Briana is expected to skip eighth grade next year. She is an involved and socially active student who is very modest about her abilities. Running track and participating in church-based activities provide a social network, but when Briana was younger, neighborhood peers did not understand why she was no longer at school with them. Briana's family has been very observant and supportive over the years and is taking special steps at this stage to keep Briana's social and academic needs in focus.

Focus Activity

Collaboration Connection...	Your Thoughts...
How could collaboration support students who do not have access to special placements?	
How have Briana's needs been met through her collaborative team?	

Diversity Link...	Your Thoughts...
How have Briana's social needs been supported in her new school?	

Focus on Inclusion...	Your Thoughts...
Why were Briana's neighborhood friends confused by her absence from school?	
How has Briana been non-academically included?	

Universal Design Application...	Your Thoughts...
How could you use the strengths of students like Briana to support their academic and social development?	
How could the needs of students like Briana be met in the general education classroom?	

𝒫 Artifact or Project Opportunities

Focus on Technology:
Create a WebQuest for a topic that might be covered in your classroom or grade-level. Continue the activity by posting your WebQuest online on the High Plains Regional Technology in Education Consortium's TrackStar system, available on their website at www.hprtec.org (a hyperlink is also available on the Companion Website).

Focus on Collaboration:
Read the article "Challenges of Identifying and Serving Gifted Children with ADHD," by Lori Flint, published in the Council for Exceptional Children's journal *Teaching Exceptional Children*, Volume 33, Number 4. The article is available online at http://journals.cec.sped.org (a direct hyperlink to the article is available on the Companion Website). Compose a reflection on the article, identifying how you will work to promote solutions to the challenges identified by the author.

Focus on Diversity:
Read the article "Underachievement Among Gifted Minority Students: Problems and Promises," by Donna Y. Ford and Antoinette Thomas, available from the ERIC Clearing House on Disabilities and Gifted Education. The article is available online at www.ericec.org (a direct link can be accessed via the Companion Website). After reading the article and reviewing the checklist and the strategies to enhance achievement among gifted minority students, describe an activity that would promote a supportive, intrinsic, or remedial goal you might have for a student. Spend time thinking about an activity that could be naturally used within an educational context that you are familiar with for an equally familiar age group.

❓ Spot Check

1. How are the needs of gifted and talented students addressed by federal legislation?

2. What is the role of individual state education systems in meeting the needs of students who are gifted?

3. What does it mean to be gifted or talented?

4. How can the classroom teacher or other educational professional support the success of a student who is gifted or talented?

Questions and Reflections

(After reading the chapter, use this area to keep track of your questions or reflections.)

⌗Standards/Topics – Project Alignment Matrix

The following professional standards are addressed in Chapter 7 within the correlating chapter topics and with the related projects or artifacts. A comprehensive matrix aligning CEC professional standards, Praxis Standards, and INTASC principles is available in the appendix of the textbook.

CEC Standards	Chapter Topics	Related Projects or Artifacts
1	• Characteristics of students who are gifted and talented. • Participating and belonging in the general education classroom. • Types of enrichment.	Focus on Diversity, Focus on Collaboration
2	• Characteristics of students who are gifted and talented. • Types of enrichment.	Focus on Collaboration, Focus on Diversity, Focus on Technology
3	• Characteristics of students who are gifted and talented. • Universally designed curriculum. • Types of enrichment. • Mentoring.	Focus on Collaboration, Focus on Diversity, Focus on Technology
4	• Participating and belonging in the general education classroom.	Focus on Collaboration, Focus on Diversity
5	• Participating and belonging in the general education classroom. • Behavioral, social, and emotional characteristics	Focus on Collaboration, Focus on Diversity
6	• Mentoring.	Focus on Diversity
7	• Participating and belonging in the general education classroom. • Universally designed curriculum. • Mentoring.	Focus on Collaboration, Focus on Technology, Focus on Diversity
10	• Collaboration. • Mentoring.	Focus on Collaboration
Praxis Standards	Chapter Topics	Related Projects or Artifacts
1	• Characteristics of students who are gifted and talented. • Participating and belonging in the general education classroom. • Behavioral, social, and emotional characteristics.	Focus on Diversity, Focus on Collaboration
2	• How students who are gifted or talented are served under IDEA.	
3	• Universally designed curriculum. • Types of enrichment.	Focus on Technology

(continued – Standards/Topics – Project Alignment Matrix)

INTASC Principles	Chapter Topics	Related Projects or Artifacts
1	• Characteristics of students who are gifted and talented. • Participating and belonging in the general education classroom. • Behavioral, social, and emotional characteristics.	Focus on Collaboration
2	• Types of enrichment. • Behavioral, social, and emotional characteristics.	Focus on Collaboration
3	• Characteristics of students who are gifted and talented. • Universally designed curriculum.	Focus on Technology
4	• Characteristics of students who are gifted and talented. • Participating and belonging in the general education classroom.	
5	• Participating and belonging in the general education classroom.	Focus on Collaboration
6	• Characteristics of students who are gifted and talented. • Universally designed curriculum.	Focus on Technology
8	• Product or process evaluation.	
9	• Collaboration.	Focus on Collaboration
10	• Collaboration. • Mentoring.	Focus on Diversity

Materials Available on the Companion Website

Self-quizzes on chapter content
Lists of available videos and class activities
Links to articles for artifact and project opportunities
Links to related websites and resources
Link to HPRTEC
Link to the article "Challenges of Identifying and Serving Gifted Children with ADHD"
Link to the article "Underachievement Among Gifted Minority Students: Problems and Promises"
Links to sample projects or artifacts
Other case study related materials to support comprehensive understanding
Graphic Organizer for Chapter 7

Chapter 8
MENTAL RETARDATION

Chapter Overview

Individuals with mental retardation experience challenges in applying skills across settings and oftentimes have difficulties with appropriate and non-appropriate behaviors. However, many individuals with mental retardation are successful in learning, interacting, and applying their skills and knowledge in their daily lives. By using functional curriculum, the educational experiences of students with mental retardation prepares them for independence; as early as elementary school, students with mental retardation can begin to master self-determination skills. In this chapter you will be introduced to definitions and characteristics of mental retardation and will be supplied information on working to support students in the general education setting.

 Don't forget to access the video and audio vignettes that accompany this chapter…

Instructional Goals

After reading this chapter you will be able to:
1. Define characteristics of mental retardation.
2. Describe different supports that may collaborate to meet the needs of students with mental retardation.
3. Understand the differences among biomedical, social, behavioral, and educational causes of mental retardation.
4. Begin to understand different assessments that are used to evaluate students with mental retardation.
5. Define self-determination.

Guiding Questions

Don't forget about the Graphic Organizer available on the Companion Website.

How do you define mental retardation?

What supports can help a student with mental retardation to be successful?

How would you describe the intellectual functioning of students with mental retardation?

What are the limitations of adaptive behavior?

What is self-determination?

What are the biomedical causes of mental retardation?

What are the social and behavioral causes of mental retardation?

How are students with mental retardation identified and evaluated?

How can the AAMR Adaptive Behavior Scale be used?

What is the self-determined learning model?

How will collaboration assist students with mental retardation?

Key Terms
In the space provided below, define the key terms in the chapter.

AAMR

Generalization

Memory

Motivation

Secondary prevention

Self-determination

Supports Intensity Scale

Tertiary prevention

Case Study and Focus Activity
Case Study Summary

Tory Woodard is a three-year-old who has experienced challenges since birth. Tory is surrounded by people who care for him and help him to overcome delays that, at this point, may very well be temporary. He has many of the skills that other children his age can boast, including signing the "alphabet song." But for Tory, his life is just beginning and at this stage, with the support and education he is receiving, the ending to his story looks nothing but positive. By using his adaptive skills he is able to get along with other children his age and communicate with his mother, teachers, and peers. Many of the challenges Tory will face lie in the limitations others may place upon him. However, with increasing expectations that Tory will be accepted and treated as an individual with strengths and weaknesses like all of us, there is the hope that Tory will live a productive, independent, and positive life in his community.

Focus Activity

Collaboration Connection...	Your Thoughts...
How will Tory's team assist in his transition into elementary school?	

(continued – Collaboration Connection ...)

How can educational professionals model the acceptance that Tory will need?	

Diversity Link...	Your Thoughts...
How will Tory be limited by societal misconceptions of his disability?	

Focus on Inclusion...	Your Thoughts...
How will Tory's non-disabled peers benefit from Tory's inclusion in the classroom, school, and community?	

Universal Design Application...	Your Thoughts...
How can the concept of Universal Design be applied to support Tory?	

Artifact or Project Opportunities

Focus on Curriculum and Instructional Choices:
Read "Mental Retardation: Update 2002" by Jack Hourcade, available from the ERIC Clearinghouse on Disabilities and Gifted Education. The direct link to the digest is http://ericec.org/digests/e637.html (a direct link is available on the Companion Website). Summarize how the changes outlined in the article relate to expectations of your students with mental retardation as a classroom teacher, educational professional, and/or facilitator of learning.

Focus on Technology:
Develop an assessment plan that is focused on the development and use of a digital portfolio to demonstrate progress of a student with mental retardation. Include the use of digital video, audio, and photographs in planning the structure of the portfolio. Student assessment plans should be attentive to demonstrating how students with mental retardation are progressing in social interaction, communication, organization, academics, and goal setting.

Focus on Diversity:
Construct a list of stereotypes that you observe being used on a daily basis. Create a reflection paper detailing how you believe those stereotypes have been developed and why they are a part of daily social interactions. In addition, compose a brief statement on how you will work with stereotypes in your role as an educational professional and what goals you have for dispelling stereotypes for all students.

❓ Spot Check

1. How has the definition of mental retardation evolved?

2. Do students with mental retardation achieve higher academic gains in inclusive or non-inclusive settings?

3. What is the self-determined learning model of instruction?

4. What are the limitations in intellectual functioning for students with mental retardation?

Questions and Reflections
(After reading the chapter, use this area to keep track of your questions or reflections.)

#Standards – Topics – Project Alignment Matrix

The following professional standards are addressed in Chapter 8 within the correlating chapter topics and with the related projects or artifacts. A comprehensive matrix aligning CEC professional standards, Praxis Standards, and INTASC principles is available in the appendix of the textbook.

CEC Standards	Chapter Topics	Related Projects or Artifacts
1	<ul><li>Intellectual functioning of students with mental retardation.</li><li>Understanding motivation.</li><li>Supports intensity scale.</li><li>Necessary supports.</li></ul>	Focus on Curriculum and Instruction, Focus on Technology, Focus on Diversity
2	<ul><li>Intellectual functioning of students with mental retardation.</li><li>Understanding motivation.</li><li>Supports intensity scale.</li><li>Necessary supports.</li></ul>	Focus on Curriculum and Instruction, Focus on Technology, Focus on Diversity
3	<ul><li>Intellectual functioning of students with mental retardation.</li><li>Academic and social progress.</li><li>Supports intensity scale.</li></ul>	Focus on Curriculum and Instruction, Focus on Technology
5	<ul><li>Academic and social progress.</li><li>Social and behavioral characteristics.</li><li>Necessary supports.</li></ul>	Focus on Curriculum and Instruction, Focus on Diversity
6	<ul><li>Self-determined learning model.</li><li>Supports intensity scale.</li></ul>	Focus on Diversity
7	<ul><li>Self-determined learning model.</li></ul>	Focus on Curriculum and Instruction
8	<ul><li>Academic and social progress.</li></ul>	Focus on Technology
10	<ul><li>Self-determined learning model.</li><li>Supports intensity scale.</li><li>Collaboration.</li></ul>	Focus on Curriculum and Instruction, Focus on Technology, Focus on Diversity
Praxis Standards	Chapter Topics	Related Projects or Artifacts
1	<ul><li>Intellectual functioning of students with mental retardation.</li><li>Academic and social progress.</li><li>Social and behavioral characteristics.</li></ul>	Focus on Curriculum and Instruction
2	<ul><li>Identification of Mental Retardation by IDEA.</li></ul>	
3	<ul><li>Understanding motivation.</li><li>Self-determined learning model.</li></ul>	Focus on Curriculum and Instruction, Focus on Technology

(continued – Standards/Topics – Project Alignment Matrix)

INTASC Principles	Chapter Topics	Related Projects or Artifacts
1	• Intellectual functioning of students with mental retardation. • Academic and social progress.	Focus on Curriculum and Instruction
2	• Social and behavioral characteristics.	
3	• Augmenting and adapting curriculum and instructional choices.	
5	• Social and behavioral characteristics.	Focus on Curriculum and Instruction, Focus on Diversity
6	• Academic and social progress.	
8	• Academic and social progress.	Focus on Technology

Materials Available on the Companion Website

Self-quizzes on chapter content

Lists of available videos and class activities

Links to related websites and resources

Links to sample projects or artifacts

Link to "Mental Retardation: Update 2002"

Other case study related materials to support comprehensive understanding

Graphic Organizer for Chapter 8

Chapter 9
SEVERE AND MULTIPLE DISABILITIES

Chapter Overview

Though there are different definitions for severe and multiple disabilities, two common characteristics are the need for a high level of support and the simultaneous presence of two or more disabilities. However, characteristics of severe and multiple disabilities are unique to every person. In this chapter, we present information that will help you understand the various causes of severe and multiple disabilities. In addition, key information on the evaluation of and support planning for persons with severe and multiple disabilities is presented.

 Don't forget to access the video and audio vignettes that accompany this chapter...

Instructional Goals

After reading this chapter you will be able to:

1. Define severe and multiple disabilities.
2. List the five major themes associated with the successful inclusion of students with severe disabilities.
3. Describe the MAPS process.
4. Define partial participation as it relates to students with severe and multiple disabilities.
5. Recall how peer tutoring can support students with disabilities.

Guiding Questions

 Don't forget about the Graphic Organizer available on the Companion Website.

How do you define severe and multiple disabilities?

What are the IDEA regulations that support students with severe and multiple disabilities?

How would you describe the intellectual functioning of students with severe and multiple disabilities?

What are the primary causes of severe and multiple disabilities?

What role does prenatal testing play in identifying severe and multiple disabilities?

What is Apgar?

How can you as a teacher promote friendships among students, including those with severe and multiple disabilities?

Key Terms
In the space provided below, define the key terms in the chapter.

Action research

Class-wide peer tutoring

Circle of inclusion

Collaborative problem solving

College connection program

MAPS process

Partial participation

Simultaneous disabilities

Case Study and Focus Activity
Case Study Summary
Joshua Spoor is a ten-year-old who has severe and multiple disabilities. Having been born with encephalocele, Joshua has developmental delays, mental retardation, seizures, and significant visual impairments. After attending the local elementary school, where he was welcomed and spent at least half of his days in the general education classroom, he is now enrolled in the local middle school. Since he lives in a nearby residential facility, Joshua's team communicates through a daily notebook that helps his family, teachers, and residential staff understand the ins and outs of his days. A strong commitment to inclusion, the opportunity for Joshua to interact with non-disabled peers on a daily basis, and the continued support of his family have provided a strong foundation on which to continue developing Joshua's independence.

Focus Activity

Collaboration Connection...	Your Thoughts...
How can educational professionals model the acceptance that Joshua will need?	

Diversity Link...	Your Thoughts...
How will Joshua be limited by societal misconceptions of his disability?	

Focus on Inclusion...	Your Thoughts...
How will Joshua's non-disabled peers benefit from his inclusion in the classroom, school, and community?	

Universal Design Application...	Your Thoughts...
How can the concept of Universal Design be applied to support Joshua?	

Artifact or Project Opportunities

Focus on Curriculum and Instructional Choices:
Using a sample lesson plan or a lesson plan you have created, restructure the lesson to include class-wide peer tutoring, being sure to include a rationale for how the tutoring improves the learning experiences of students with severe and multiple disabilities.

Focus on Technology:
Use Internet-based resources to develop a WebQuest to teach and train students to participate in class-wide peer tutoring. Visit the Trackstar webpage at http://trackstar.hprtec.org for examples of WebQuests and other materials.

Focus on Collaboration:
Compose a letter addressed to the parents of the students with whom you plan to work. In the letter, identify how you plan to communicate with them, in what ways you would like their input on the education of their child, and your perspective on how parents and teachers can collaborate.

Spot Check

1. How are severe and multiple disabilities defined differently under IDEA?

2. How is intellectual functioning measured?

3. What are adaptive skills?

4. What are prenatal biomedical factors and how are they connected with severe or multiple disabilities?

5. What prenatal testing can help identify and prevent multiple disabilities?

6. What is the MAPS process?

Questions and Reflections
(After reading the chapter, use this area to keep track of your questions or reflections.)

⌗Standards/Topics – Project Alignment Matrix

The following professional standards are addressed in Chapter 9 within the correlating chapter topics and with the related projects or artifacts. A comprehensive matrix aligning CEC professional standards, Praxis Standards, and INTASC principles is available in the appendix of the textbook.

CEC Standards	Chapter Topics	Related Projects or Artifacts
1	• Defining severe and multiple disabilities. • Extent of support. • Self-care skills.	Focus on Curriculum and Instruction, Focus on Technology
2	• Defining severe and multiple disabilities. • Extent of support. • Intellectual functioning and academic skills. • Promoting friendships. • Self-care skills. • Circle of inclusion.	Focus on Collaboration
3	• Defining severe and multiple disabilities. • Extent of support. • Intellectual functioning and academic skills. • Circle of inclusion.	Focus on Technology
4	• Collaboration. • Partnerships.	Focus on Collaboration, Focus on Curriculum and Instruction, Focus on Technology
5	• Extent of support. • Promoting friendships. • Self-care skills. • Circle of inclusion.	Focus on Curriculum and Instruction, Focus on Technology
6	• Communication skills. • Collaborative partnerships. • College connection program.	Focus on Collaboration
7	• Planning a universally designed learning environment. • College connection program. • Circle of inclusion.	Focus on Curriculum and Instruction, Focus on Technology
8	• Extent of support. • Planning a universally designed learning environment. • College connection program.	Focus on Curriculum and Instruction, Focus on Technology
9	• Planning a universally designed learning environment.	Focus on Curriculum and Instruction
10	• Extent of support. • Communication skills. • Collaborative partnerships. • College connection program.	Focus on Collaboration

(continued – Standards/Topics – Project Alignment Matrix)

Praxis Standards	Chapter Topics	Related Projects or Artifacts
1	• Defining severe and multiple disabilities. • Intellectual functioning and academic skills. • Adaptive skills.	Focus on Curriculum and Instruction, Focus on Technology
2	• IDEA regulations. • Simultaneous disabilities.	
3	• Planning a universally designed learning environment. • Partnerships and collaboration.	Focus on Curriculum and Instruction, Focus on Technology, Focus on Collaboration
INTASC Principles	**Chapter Topics**	**Related Projects or Artifacts**
1	• Intellectual functioning and academic skills. • Adaptive skills.	Focus on Curriculum and Instruction
2	• Intellectual functioning. • Peer tutoring.	Focus on Technology
3	• Adapting curriculum and instructional choices. • Planning a universally designed learning environment.	Focus on Collaboration
4	• Peer tutoring. • Class-wide peer tutoring.	Focus on Curriculum and Instruction, Focus on Technology
5	• Peer tutoring. • Promoting friendships.	Focus on Curriculum and Instruction, Focus on Technology
6	• Collaboration and partnering for success.	Focus on Collaboration
7	• Planning a universally designed learning environment. • MAPS process.	
10	• Partnerships and collaboration.	Focus on Collaboration

Materials Available on the Companion Website

Self-quizzes on chapter content

Lists of available videos and class activities

Links to related websites and resources

Links to sample projects or artifacts

Other case study related materials to support comprehensive understanding

Graphic Organizer for Chapter 9

Chapter 10
AUTISM

Chapter Overview

Autism is a developmental disability that can significantly affect an individual in your classroom. Ranging from verbal communication to educational performance, autism can change the way a student interacts with their environment, as well as their peers. Students with autism can benefit from simple additions and accommodations in the classroom setting. As autism is part of a larger category of pervasive developmental disorders, this chapter will introduce you to related disorders such as Asperger's Syndrome, common characteristics and causes of autism, instructional approaches and curriculum designs that can benefit the learning goals of the autistic student, and positive behavioral supports that can be implemented at several different levels to support students in the classroom, school, and larger community.

 Don't forget to access the video and audio vignettes that accompany this chapter...

Instructional Goals

After reading this chapter you will be able to:
1. Describe characteristics of autism.
2. Discuss and understand how autism is identified and what causes have been linked to autism.
3. Identify the needs of an autistic student in the classroom and larger community.
4. Understand the benefits of collaboration and communication across settings.
5. Connect knowledge to specific case studies.
6. Discuss and understand how instructional and curricular choices can support students with autism in progressing through the general education curriculum.

Guiding Questions

Don't forget about the Graphic Organizer available on the Companion Website.

How are students with autism identified?

How does language development differ for students with autism?

How does social development impact students with autism?

What are some identifying causes of autism?

How are students with autism evaluated?

In what ways can collaboration support the learning and social goals of students with autism?

How can transition help students in their planning?

Key Terms

In the space provided below, define the key terms in the chapter.

Asperger's syndrome

Echolalia

Environmental predictability

Pervasive developmental disorder

Positive behavioral support

Repetitive behavior

Case Study and Focus Activity

Case Study Summary

Jeremy Jones is a thirteen-year-old middle school student in Kansas City. Jeremy is the only student at his school with autism, but the interventions and supports that have been put in place for Jeremy have undoubtedly benefited the entire school. Jeremy has a keen memory and an undeniable talent for mapping out his hometown. He has been involved with his church community and has a supportive home environment. Jeremy makes an effort to use what he knows about "appropriate social behavior" when interacting with peers and teachers at school, but he still has challenging moments. Repetitive behaviors and a need for routine often pose challenges, but Jeremy's strengths in remembering names, dates, and places create an opportunity for him in the classroom. Jeremy has a strong network of individuals working with him, using positive behavioral supports and other systems of interventions to insure his success.

Focus Activity

Collaboration Connection...	Your Thoughts...
How has Jeremy been supported at home, in the community, and at school?	
How has Jeremy's presence at Central Middle School changed the approach Central takes regarding behavior or discipline?	

Diversity Link...	Your Thoughts...
In what ways can Jeremy's strengths be used to include him into the greater community?	

(continued – Diversity Link ...)

How can Jeremy's social needs be met?	

Focus on Inclusion...	Your Thoughts...
How have Jeremy's teachers included him in the general education classroom?	
How has Jeremy learned from his non-disabled peers?	

Universal Design Application...	Your Thoughts...
How can a universally designed learning environment support Jeremy in his academic learning and social goals?	

Artifact or Project Opportunities

Focus on Curriculum and Instructional Choices:
Using the cooperative learning activity found on the Companion Website, augment the activity so that it will support Jeremy in successfully communicating and collaborating with peers in the general education classroom.

Focus on Technology:
Using what you know about Jeremy's strengths and interests, identify types of technology that could be used in the classroom. After identifying at least three types, explain how you could use each in the classroom, what type of training will be needed to insure Jeremy's understanding and successful use of the technology, and how you could communicate the availability of the technology to other professionals who are supporting Jeremy.

Focus on Collaboration:
Imagine that you have been asked to coordinate the supports that Jeremy is receiving at school, home, and in the community. Using the communication plan found on the Companion Website, develop a plan for communicating with the multiple stakeholders involved in Jeremy's education.

❓Spot Check

1. What are the major characteristics associated with autism?

2. Describe the causes of autism presented in the chapter.

3. Why is it important to be attentive to setting events when working with the problem behavior of a student with autism?

4. What is a functional assessment and how can it be used to support the classroom planning of a teacher?

5. How can the social skills of students with autism be supported in the classroom?

Questions and Reflections
(After reading the chapter, use this area to keep track of your questions or reflections.)

⌗Standards/Topics – Project Alignment Matrix

The following professional standards are addressed in Chapter 10 within the correlating chapter topics and with the related projects or artifacts. A comprehensive matrix aligning CEC professional standards, Praxis Standards, and INTASC principles is available in the appendix of the textbook.

CEC Standards	Chapter Topics	Related Projects or Artifacts
1	• Characteristics of autism.	Focus on Collaboration, Focus on Technology
2	• Characteristics of autism. • Instructional decision making to insure progress in the general education curriculum for students with autism. • Evaluating students with autism. • Repetitive behavior. • Curricular and instructional needs of students with autism. • Post-secondary transition needs.	Focus on Curriculum and Instruction, Focus on Collaboration
3	• Characteristics of autism. • Instructional decision making to insure progress in the general education curriculum for students with autism. • Curricular and instructional needs of students with autism. • Augmenting curriculum and instruction.	Focus on Curriculum and Instruction, Focus on Technology
4	• Collaboration to meet student needs. • Curricular and instructional needs of students with autism. • Augmenting curriculum and instruction.	Focus on Technology, Focus on Curriculum and Instruction
5	• Instructional decision making to insure progress in the general education curriculum for students with autism. • Repetitive behavior. • Environmental predictability.	Focus on Curriculum and Instructional
6	• Collaborative relationships. • Post-secondary transition needs.	Focus on Collaboration
7	• Instructional decision making to insure progress in the general education curriculum for students with autism. • Environmental predictability. • Curricular and instructional needs of students with autism. • Augmenting curriculum and instruction.	Focus on Technology, Focus on Curriculum and Instruction
8	• Evaluating students with autism. • Curricular and instructional needs of students with autism.	Focus on Collaboration, Focus on Technology

(continued – Standards/Topics – Projects Alignment Matrix)

	Chapter Topics	
9	• Evaluating students with autism.	Focus on Collaboration, Focus on Technology
10	• Collaborative relationships. • Post-secondary transition needs.	Focus on Collaboration
Praxis Standards	**Chapter Topics**	**Related Projects or Artifacts**
1	• Characteristics of autism. • Defining autism.	Focus on Curriculum and Instructional
2	• Historical and biomedical causes.	
3	• Collaborative relationships. • Collaboration to support instruction. • Specific instructional choices for students with autism.	Focus on Collaboration
INTASC Principles	**Chapter Topics**	**Related Projects or Artifacts**
1	• Progress in the general curriculum.	Focus on Curriculum and Instructional
2	• Historical causes of autism.	Focus on Technology
3	• Augmenting curriculum.	Focus on Technology
5	• Social development. • Environmental predictability.	
8	• Evaluating students with autism.	
9		Focus on Collaboration
10	• Related services. • Collaboration to meet student needs.	Focus on Curriculum and Instructional, Focus on Collaboration, Focus on Technology

Materials Available on the Companion Website

Self-quizzes on chapter content

Communication plan and cooperative learning activity

Links to related websites and resources

Maps and other materials created by Jeremy and used to support Jeremy

Positive behavioral support plans

Information and resources on Asperger's Syndrome

Information and resources on positive behavioral supports

Graphic Organizer for Chapter 10

Chapter 11
OTHER HEALTH IMPAIRMENTS

Chapter Overview

Understanding how health impairments affect students in your classroom is the first step to providing meaningful inclusion and instruction. In this chapter other health impairments will be addressed with attention to strengths as well as limits. Specific health impairments such as sickle cell, epilepsy, cancer, asthma, and human immunodeficiency virus among others are presented. Both social and academic needs of students are addressed.

 Don't forget to access the video and audio vignettes that accompany this chapter...

Instructional Goals

After reading this chapter you will be able to:
1. Describe characteristics of Other Health Impairments.
2. Understand the causes of Other Health Impairments.
3. Describe evaluation processes for students with Other Health Impairments.
4. Reflect on the importance of inclusion for students with Other Health Impairments.
5. Understand the curricular and instructional needs.

Guiding Questions

Don't forget about the Graphic Organizer available on the Companion Website.

What are Other Health Impairments?

Why is it important to address the individuality of conditions?

How are strength, vitality, and alertness connected to identifying other health impairments?

What is sickle cell disease?

What are the characteristics of sickle cell disease?

What are some of the classroom needs of students with sickle cell disease?

What are the social and emotional needs of students with sickle cell disease?

What is epilepsy?

What are the classroom needs of students with epilepsy?

What are some environmental triggers of seizures?

What is asthma and how does it affect students in the classroom?

How can an action plan support students with asthma?

What affects can treatments for cancer have on students?

Why are positive social interactions important for students with cancer?

How can the teacher's perceptions affect the inclusion of a student with cancer?

How can open discussions support students with diabetes?

What is human immunodeficiency virus?

Why is confidentiality important for students with human immunodeficiency virus?

What are cultural issues associated with human immunodeficiency virus?

What are the different causes of human immunodeficiency virus?

How are cognitive, academic, and behavioral influences considered when evaluating a student for Other Health Impairments?

How can a health care plan be included as part of the support students receive?

Why would it be important to avoid retention?

Key Terms

In the space provided below, define the key terms in the chapter.

Absence seizures

Acute condition

Airway hyperresponsiveness

Anemia

Chronic condition

Epilepsy

Homebound placement

Hyperglycemia

Hypoglycemia

Leukemia

Ketoacidosis

Mild intermittent

Moderate persistent

Myoclonic

Partial seizures

Respite care

Sickle cell disease

Severe persistent

Toni-clonic seizures

Case Study and Focus Activity

Case Study Summary

Kyle Edwards is a ten-year-old with sickle cell disease. Kyle struggles with episodes of excruciating pain but makes every effort to maintain a positive attitude. Even at his young age, he knows how to handle the pain sickle cell causes him. Luckily, he has the strong support of family and community members, some of whom share his personal understanding of sickle cell since they too have suffered from the disease for years. Showing compassion for others, Kyle is courageous and wise well beyond his years. Kyle's fourth-grade teacher is able to send work via fax to teachers at the local hospital who can make sure that he doesn't fall behind his classmates.

Focus Activity

Collaboration Connection...	Your Thoughts...
How has Kyle been supported throughout the community?	

Diversity Link...	Your Thoughts...
How is Kyle interacting with his peers?	

Focus on Inclusion...	Your Thoughts...
In what ways can Kyle be included in the community and school?	

(continued – Focus on Inclusion ...)

Why has the hospital taken on the challenge of providing teaching staff on site?	

Universal Design Application...	Your Thoughts...
How is Kyle's learning affected by sickle cell disease?	

Artifact or Project Opportunities

Focus on Technology:
Visit the Companion Website, specifically the web links for Chapter 11. Choose one health impairment (asthma, HIV, epilepsy, cancer, or diabetes) and investigate its associated issues in further detail. Then use the information you have found to create an information sheet on that impairment. The information sheet should focus on causes, number of students generally affected, care needs, and safety issues.

Focus on Collaboration:
Using information provided in the text, write a letter that could be used to communicate with persons inside and outside of the school who are providing support services to students with other health impairments. The letter should explain how you plan to convey information, ways in which you will participate in providing supports to the student, and how you would like to handle any times of crisis or hospitalization.

Focus on Diversity:
Using the information in the textbook, develop a position statement on including students with other health impairments in the classroom. Make sure that each statement is attentive to personal beliefs, concerns, and readiness.

Spot Check

1. In what forms are Other Health Impairments usually present in schools?

2. How can students with OHI be included in the general education classroom?

3. What are the social needs of students with OHI?

4. How should you approach communication with peers regarding information or concerns about a student's health?

5. In what ways can you ensure progress through the general education curriculum for students with OHI?

Questions and Reflections
(After reading the chapter, use this area to keep track of your questions or reflections.)

⌗ Standards/Topics – Project Alignment Matrix

The following professional standards are addressed in Chapter 11 within the correlating chapter topics and with the related projects or artifacts. A comprehensive matrix aligning CEC professional standards, Praxis Standards, and INTASC principles is available in the appendix of the textbook.

CEC Standards	Chapter Topics	Related Projects or Artifacts
1	<ul><li>Individuality of impairments.</li><li>Limitations of health conditions.</li><li>Environmental triggers of epilepsy.</li><li>Effects of cancer treatments on student behavior, functioning, and health.</li><li>Preventing students with other health impairments from dropping out of school.</li><li>Promoting school safety.</li></ul>	Focus on Technology, Focus on Diversity, Focus on Collaboration
2	<ul><li>Individuality of impairments.</li><li>Limitations of health conditions.</li><li>Social and emotional needs of students with other health impairments.</li><li>Environmental triggers of epilepsy.</li><li>Relaxation techniques.</li><li>Learning and behavior of students with HIV.</li><li>Sharing information regarding student health impairments with peers.</li><li>Effects of cancer treatments on student behavior, functioning, and health.</li><li>Creating an action plan for meeting the classroom needs of students with other health impairments.</li><li>Learned helplessness and students with other health impairments.</li><li>Promoting school safety.</li></ul>	Focus on Technology, Focus on Diversity, Focus on Collaboration
3	<ul><li>Individuality of impairments.</li><li>Augmenting curriculum and instruction.</li><li>Creating an action plan for meeting the classroom needs of students with other health impairments.</li><li>Learned helplessness and students with other health impairments.</li></ul>	Focus on Technology, Focus on Collaboration
4	<ul><li>Sharing information regarding student health impairments with peers.</li></ul>	Focus on Technology

(continued – Standards/Topics – Projects Alignment Matrix)

	Chapter Topics	Related Projects or Artifacts
5	• Classroom needs of students with other health impairments. • Universally designed learning. • Social and emotional needs of students with other health impairments. • Environmental triggers of epilepsy. • Relaxation techniques. • Learning and behavior of students with HIV. • Sharing information regarding student health impairments with peers.	Focus on Technology
6	• Creating an action plan for meeting the classroom needs of students with other health impairments. • Encouraging open discussions with students with other health impairments. • Preventing students with other health impairments from dropping out of school.	Focus on Collaboration, Focus on Technology, Focus on Diversity
7	• Universally designed learning. • Augmenting curriculum and instruction. • Encouraging open discussions with students with other health impairments. • Preventing students with other health impairments from dropping out of school.	Focus on Collaboration, Focus on Technology
8	• Augmenting curriculum and instruction.	Focus on Collaboration
9	• Limitations of health conditions. • Learning and behavior of students with HIV. • Sharing information regarding student health impairments with peers. • Preventing students with other health impairments from dropping out of school. • Promoting school safety.	Focus on Collaboration, Focus on Technology
10	• Classroom needs of students with other health impairments. • Creating an action plan for meeting the classroom needs of students with other health impairments. • Preventing students with other health impairments from dropping out of school.	Focus on Collaboration, Focus on Technology, Focus on Diversity
Praxis Standards	**Chapter Topics**	**Related Projects or Artifacts**
1	• Individuality of impairments. • Universally designed learning.	Focus on Technology
2	• Definition of other health impairments. • Confidentiality in some other health impairments.	Focus on Technology

(continued – Standards/Topics – Projects Alignment Matrix)

3	• Limitations of health conditions. • Collaboration to support instruction. • Specific instructional choices for students with autism.	Focus on Technology
INTASC Principles	**Chapter Topics**	**Related Projects or Artifacts**
1	• Progress in the general curriculum.	Focus on Collaboration
2	• Peer-led discussions on HIV. • Progress in the general curriculum.	Focus on Technology
3	• Augmenting curriculum.	
5	• Social development. • Environmental predictability.	Focus on Technology, Focus on Collaboration
7	• Progress in the general curriculum.	
8	• Cognitive evaluation of students with other health impairments.	
9		Focus on Diversity
10	• Encouraging open discussions with students with other health impairments. • Peer led discussions on HIV. • Action planning for providing services.	Focus on Technology

Materials Available on the Companion Website

Self-quizzes on chapter content

Links to related websites and resources

Information and resources on sickle cell disease

Information and resources on diabetes

Information and resources on asthma

Information and resources on cancer

Information and resources on epilepsy

Link to Starlight Foundation's website at www.starlight.org

Link to kidshealth.org website

Graphic Organizer for Chapter 11

Chapter 12
PHYSICAL DISABILITIES

Chapter Overview

In this chapter you will be introduced to physical disabilities. Understanding how various educational professionals will interact with students who have physical disabilities is an important first step to effective collaboration and successful student progression through the general education curriculum. Characteristics and definitions are followed by information on related assistive technologies and curricular approaches that support students in the classroom and school contexts.

 Don't forget to access the video and audio vignettes that accompany this chapter...

Instructional Goals

After reading this chapter you will be able to:
1. Understand the prevalence of physical disabilities.
2. Describe how students with physical disabilities can be evaluated.
3. Reflect on the assistive technologies available to support communication and mobility.
4. Understand how students with disabilities can be included in the general education curriculum.

Guiding Questions

Don't forget about the Graphic Organizer available on the Companion Website.

What is the definition of a physical disability?

What are the characteristics of cerebral palsy?

What are the four types of cerebral palsy?

What is spina bifida?

What are the three common forms of spina bifida?

What is muscular dystrophy?

What is an Apgar screening?

Key Terms

In the space provided below, define the key terms in the chapter.

Assistive technology in mobility

Assistive technology in communication

Cerebral palsy

Incontinence

Muscular dystrophy

Perinatal

Prenatal

Postnatal

Spina bifida

Case Study and Focus Activity

Case Study Summary

Rommel Nanasca is a high school student who has a physical disability. He attends school, where he is provided supports by therapists and other related service professionals. Rommel has strong support from his mother, and together they meet the challenges and successes head on. He goes to school in a wheelchair and a flexible plastic vest that helps support his upper body. The routines that Rommel and his mother go through provide him the extra support he needs to be productive and healthy.

Focus Activity

Collaboration Connection...	Your Thoughts...
How are Rommel's needs met by multiple people?	
Has collaboration helped Rommel? If so, how?	

Diversity Link...	Your Thoughts...
How can students with needs similar to Rommel's be included both socially and academically in the school environment?	

Focus on Inclusion...	Your Thoughts...
Are there any challenges in including students with needs like Rommel's in the school environment? What are the challenges and who is responsible for meeting them?	

Universal Design Application...	Your Thoughts...
How can universally designed buildings support the needs of students like Rommel?	
In what ways are the design components of a universally designed building utilized in a school context?	

Artifact or Project Opportunities

Focus on Curriculum and Instructional Choices:

Imagine that you have the same physical limitations as Rommel. After attending a school- or work-related meeting (such as a class), reflect on how your ability to participate in those events would differ if you were Rommel. Explain, via a written reflection, what changes would have to be made in order for you to be successful.

Focus on Technology:

Visit the Assistive Technology Training Online project (ATTO) at http://atto.buffalo.edu. By choosing the "tutorials" option you can complete a tutorial on any of the listed products. After completing a tutorial, develop a product review, being specifically attentive to how that product could be used in your classroom and how it could assist in the learning or teaching of students with disabilities.

Focus on Diversity:

Visit a local mall, grocery story, or other service establishment. During your visit, assess the establishment for meeting the architectural requirements of universal design. To access a list of universal design principles for environments and products, check out the Center for Universal Design online at www.design.ncsu.edu:8120/cud (a direct link to this website is available on the Companion Website). After you return from your visit, compose a report on how the establishment is constructed to meet the needs of individuals with physical disabilities, and how the establishment's physical setup could be improved.

Spot Check

1. What are the four types of cerebral palsy identified in the text?

2. What are the three forms of spina bifida presented in the text?

3. What changes in curricular and instructional choices will support students with physical disabilities in the classroom?

4. How can collaboration support the successful inclusion of students with physical disabilities?

Questions and Reflections

(After reading the chapter, use this area to keep track of your questions or reflections.)

⌗Standards/Topics – Project Alignment Matrix

The following professional standards are addressed in Chapter 12 within the correlating chapter topics and with the related projects or artifacts. A comprehensive matrix aligning CEC professional standards, Praxis Standards, and INTASC principles is available in the appendix of the textbook.

CEC Standards	Chapter Topics	Related Projects or Artifacts
1	• Defining physical disabilities. • Causes of physical disabilities.	Focus on Curriculum and Instruction, Focus on Technology
2	• Defining physical disabilities. • Causes of physical disabilities. • Different types and forms of physical disabilities.	Focus on Curriculum and Instruction, Focus on Technology, Focus on Diversity
3	• Defining physical disabilities. • Causes of physical disabilities. • Different types and forms of physical disabilities. • Collaborating to meet the needs of students with physical disabilities.	Focus on Curriculum and Instruction, Focus on Technology, Focus on Diversity
5	• Causes of physical disabilities. • Collaborating to meet the needs of students with physical disabilities.	Focus on Diversity
8	• Evaluation of students with physical disabilities.	Focus on Curriculum and Instruction
9	• Causes of physical disabilities.	
10	• Collaborating to meet the needs of students with physical disabilities.	Focus on Diversity, Focus on Technology
Praxis Standards	Chapter Topics	Related Projects or Artifacts
1	• Defining physical disabilities. • Causes of physical disabilities. • Conditions associated with physical disabilities.	Focus on Curriculum and Instruction, Focus on Technology
2	• Understanding the presence of physical disabilities.	
3	• Evaluation of students with physical disabilities. • Extent of services.	Focus on Diversity

(continued – Standards/Topics – Project Alignment Matrix)

INTASC Principles	Chapter Topics	Related Projects or Artifacts
1	• Including students in the general education curriculum.	Focus on Curriculum and Instruction, Focus on Technology, Focus on Diversity
2	• Including students in the general education curriculum.	Focus on Curriculum and Instruction
3	• Including students in the general education curriculum.	
5	• Curricular adaptations and assistive technology.	Focus on Technology
8	• Evaluation of students with physical disabilities.	Focus on Diversity
10	• Collaboration.	Focus on Curriculum and Instruction

Materials Available on the Companion Website

Self-quizzes on chapter content

Lists of available videos and class activities

Links to related websites and resources

Links to sample projects or artifacts

Other case study related materials to support comprehensive understanding

Graphic Organizer for Chapter 12

Chapter 13
TRAUMATIC BRAIN INJURY

Chapter Overview

This chapter presents an overview of traumatic brain injury. Traumatic brain injury can affect an individual's academic, emotional, and social abilities. It is important that educational professionals are aware of the needs of students with TBI, in order to make transitions smooth and to have appropriate expectations. After learning specific characteristics and definitions, you will be presented with information on how to successfully include students with TBI. Careful attention is given to the immediacy of services and the need for social and academic intervention.

 Don't forget to access the video and audio vignettes that accompany this chapter...

Instructional Goals

After reading this chapter you will be able to:
1. Describe how traumatic brain injury can affect a student's social, academic, and emotional abilities.
2. Recall effective teaching practices for working with students with traumatic brain injury.
3. Understand how to encourage participation.
4. Describe strategies that would be helpful to the transition of students with TBI.

Guiding Questions

Don't forget about the Graphic Organizer available on the Companion Website.

How is Traumatic Brain Injury covered by IDEA?

What are the physical changes associated with TBI?

What are the cognitive changes associated with TBI?

What the linguistic changes are associated with TBI?

What observations might be made about social, behavioral, and personality changes for students with TBI?

How is TBI evaluated?

How can the concepts of universal design be used to support the needs of students with TBI?

Key Terms

In the space provided below, define the key terms in the chapter.

Aphasia

Closed head injury

Cognitive retraining

Open head injury

Traumatic brain injury

Case Study and Focus Activity

Case Study Summary

Jarris Garner is a ten-year-old who was involved in a serious car accident at the age of seven months. Having uncertainties about Jarris's health immediately following the accident, her family made the decision that Jarris would live with her grandmother. There she would be able to get one-on-one attention, and her mother could work with her on redeveloping the communication skills that were lost with her injuries. Jarris began participating in the Language Acquisition Program and successfully learned skills to promote social, behavioral, and communication skills. Now ten years old, Jarris is successful at school and is continuing to make progress.

Focus Activity

Collaboration Connection...	Your Thoughts...
How can a traumatic brain injury change the role of individuals who are involved in some way in the life of the student?	
How much should the school be involved in helping to communicate the needs, progress, or struggles of a student across environments?	

Diversity Link...	Your Thoughts...
How can the social life or social skills of a student change after a traumatic brain injury?	

Focus on Inclusion...	Your Thoughts...
In what ways will high expectations affect the inclusion of a student with a traumatic brain injury?	
Universal Design Application...	Your Thoughts...

Should the classroom environment (academic or social) change to meet the needs of students with a traumatic brain injury? Why or why not?	

Artifact or Project Opportunities

Focus on Curriculum and Instructional Choices:
Develop a guide that a student with TBI could use to navigate a social interaction such as lunch, a sporting event, or a conversation. Be sure to include the what, when, where, how, and who of the social interaction and explain how you would teach the student with TBI to utilize the guide.

Focus on Technology:
Design a communication plan that utilizes technology. In theory this communication plan would assist in keeping communication lines open between the stakeholders involved in the education of a student with TBI, but could be generalized to include other students. The communication plan should be accessible daily, utilize technologies that are available, and supply necessary equipment to all stakeholders. Make sure that a list of training needed to implement the communication plan, a budget that outlines the needs of the plan, and expected outcomes are included.

Spot Check

1. Does IDEA cover all types of TBI?

2. What are the four areas of change that are often observed?

3. What strategies can assist students with TBI?

4. What are the three major causes of TBI?

Questions and Reflections
(After reading the chapter, use this area to keep track of your questions or reflections.)

⌗Standards/Topics – Project Alignment Matrix

The following professional standards are addressed in Chapter 13 within the correlating chapter topics and with the related projects or artifacts. A comprehensive matrix aligning CEC professional standards, Praxis Standards, and INTASC principles is available in the appendix of the textbook.

CEC Standards	Chapter Topics	Related Projects or Artifacts
1	<ul><li>Characteristics of traumatic brain injury.</li><li>Defining traumatic brain injury.</li><li>Types of traumatic brain injury.</li><li>Self-advocacy.</li><li>Understanding physical, cognitive, linguistic, and other changes.</li></ul>	Focus on Technology
2	<ul><li>Characteristics of traumatic brain injury.</li><li>Defining traumatic brain injury.</li><li>Types of traumatic brain injury.</li><li>Self-advocacy.</li><li>Understanding physical, cognitive, linguistic, and other changes.</li></ul>	Focus on Curriculum and Instruction
4	<ul><li>Characteristics of traumatic brain injury.</li><li>Types of traumatic brain injury.</li><li>Providing supports to meet individual student needs.</li><li>Collaborating to meet the needs of students across environments.</li><li>Understanding physical, cognitive, linguistic, and other changes.</li></ul>	Focus on Technology, Focus on Curriculum and Instruction
5	<ul><li>Social, personality, and behavioral changes associated with traumatic brain injury.</li><li>Self-advocacy.</li><li>Providing supports to meet individual student needs.</li><li>Understanding physical, cognitive, linguistic, and other changes.</li></ul>	Focus on Curriculum and Instruction
6	<ul><li>Social, personality, and behavioral changes associated with traumatic brain injury.</li><li>Collaborating to meet the needs of students across environments.</li></ul>	Focus on Technology
7	<ul><li>Self-advocacy.</li><li>Providing supports to meet individual student needs.</li><li>Understanding physical, cognitive, linguistic, and other changes.</li></ul>	Focus on Technology

(continued – Standards/Topics – Project Alignment Matrix)

8	• Evaluating students and determining the presence of a traumatic brain injury.	
9	• Understanding physical, cognitive, linguistic, and other changes.	Focus on Curriculum and Instruction
10	• Social, personality, and behavioral changes associated with traumatic brain injury. • Collaborating to meet the needs of students across environments.	Focus on Curriculum and Instruction
Praxis Standards	**Chapter Topics**	**Related Projects or Artifacts**
1	• Characteristics of blindness and low vision. • Causes of blindness and low vision.	Focus on Curriculum and Instruction
2	• Coverage of traumatic brain injury under IDEA.	
3	• Nature and extent of services. • Specialized instructional supports.	Focus on Technology
INTASC Principles	**Chapter Topics**	**Related Projects or Artifacts**
1	• Augmenting curriculum.	
2	• Augmenting curriculum. • Understanding physical, cognitive, linguistic, and other changes.	Focus on Curriculum and Instruction
3	• Specialized instructional supports.	
4	• Processing and other changes associated with traumatic brain injury.	Focus on Curriculum and Instruction
6	• Developing a universally designed learning environment.	
8	• Evaluating students and determining the presence of a traumatic brain injury.	Focus on Technology
10	• Collaborating to meet the needs of students across environments.	Focus on Technology

Materials Available on the Companion Website

Self-quizzes on chapter content

Links to related websites and resources

Discussion starters

Links to sample projects or artifacts

Other case study related materials to support comprehensive understanding

PowerPoint Presentation for Chapter 13

Graphic Organizer for Chapter 13

Chapter 14
COMMUNICATION DISORDERS

Chapter Overview

It is important to take some time to understand the simple ways that communication supports our daily interactions and how communication disorders affect those naturally occurring interactions for some individuals. In this chapter you will be introduced to communication disorders. Through connecting the needs of students with communication disorders, you will learn about the curricular and instructional needs of individuals with communication disorders and be provided with information on how those individuals can be supported in the classroom, school, and community.

 Don't forget to access the video and audio vignettes that accompany this chapter...

Instructional Goals

After reading this chapter you will be able to:
1. Describe how students with communication disorders are supported in the general education curriculum.
2. Understand cultural diversity in communication.
3. Reflect on how communication disorders can be accommodated in the general curriculum.
4. Describe the role of a speech-language pathologist in evaluating students with communication disorders.

Guiding Questions

Don't forget about the Graphic Organizer available on the Companion Website.

How do you define communication disorders?

What is the difference between a speech or language disorder and a dialect?

What are the differences and similarities among the following: speech disorders, articulation disorders, voice disorders, and fluency disorders?

Describe the Social Interaction theories associated with communication disorders.

What are the primary causes of communication disorders?

What is the difference between an organic disorder and a functional disorder?

Who evaluates communications disorders? What types of assessments are employed?

How can you adapt or augment instruction to include students with communication disorders?

Key Terms

In the space provided below, define the key terms in the chapter.

Apraxia of speech

Augmentative and alternative communication systems

Bilingual evaluation

Holistic viewpoint

Phonology

Pragmatics

Morphology

Syntax

Semantics

Standardized articulation

Case Study and Focus Activity

Case Study Summary

George Wedge is a kindergarten student who was born with a condition known as Dandy Walker syndrome. He has been involved with non-disabled peers in preschool environments and is progressing well through kindergarten. George uses a device to augment communication and, like other children his age, enjoys taking art classes, reading, and playing with his classmates, peers, and brother. His support system is filled with individuals who hold high expectations for him and want to learn more in order to include and support him in his learning and living. George still has to master some skills, such as swallowing and shaping words, but has experienced a great deal of success so far.

Focus Activity

Collaboration Connection...	Your Thoughts...
How has George's support system encouraged him to have high expectations for himself?	

Diversity Link...	Your Thoughts...
How has George's presence in the classroom allowed non-disabled peers the opportunity to learn from him?	

Focus on Inclusion...	Your Thoughts...
Why has George been included in environments with non-disabled peers since such an early age?	

Universal Design Application...	Your Thoughts...
How can George's academic needs be met?	

Artifact or Project Opportunities

Focus on Curriculum and Instructional Choices:
Using the rubric creation tool Rubristar (available online at http://rubistar.4teachers.org), create a rubric that could be used to assess a student's oral presentation. Augment that rubric to accommodate the needs of students with communication delays.

Focus on Technology:
Using the information found on the National Information Center for Children and Youth with Disabilities website concerning speech and language impairments (available online at http://www.nichcy.org/pubs/factshe/fs11txt.htm#edimps) create a fact sheet presentation using presentation software such as PowerPoint. Summarize this fact sheet so that it answers two key questions: (1) what is a communication disorder? and (2) what are the educational implications for students with a communication disorder?

Focus on Diversity:
After visiting a local school, classroom, or library, create a reflection of that visit that answers the following questions: (1) how was the school, classroom, or library designed to meet the needs of individuals with communication disorders, (2) what improvements could be made to create a more "user friendly" environment for students with communication disorders, (3) how was the environment designed to make essential support or augmentation a natural part of a student's interaction, and (4) what struggles would an individual with a communication disorder encounter in this environment?

Spot Check

1. What are the differences between speech disorders and a language disorder?

2. How would you define dialects?

3. What is an articulation disorder?

4. How are qualitative and quantitative measures used to evaluate students for communication disorders?

5. How can students use augmentative and alternative communication systems to support their learning?

Questions and Reflections
(After reading the chapter, use this area to keep track of your questions or reflections.)

#Standards/Topics – Project Alignment Matrix

The following professional standards are addressed in Chapter 14 within the correlating chapter topics and with the related projects or artifacts. A comprehensive matrix aligning CEC professional standards, Praxis Standards, and INTASC principles is available in the appendix of the textbook.

CEC Standards	Chapter Topics	Related Projects or Artifacts
1	<ul><li>Characteristics of communication disorders.</li><li>Characteristics of language impairments.</li><li>Self-advocacy.</li><li>Functional communication disorders.</li><li>Organic communication disorders.</li></ul>	Focus on Technology
2	<ul><li>Characteristics of communication disorders.</li><li>Defining speech and language disorders.</li><li>Characteristics of language impairments.</li><li>Self-advocacy.</li><li>Functional communication disorders.</li><li>Organic communication disorders.</li></ul>	Focus on Diversity, Focus on Curriculum and Instruction
3	<ul><li>Characteristics of communication disorders.</li><li>Defining speech and language disorders.</li><li>Characteristics of language impairments.</li><li>Self-advocacy.</li></ul>	Focus on Technology, Focus on Curriculum and Instruction, Focus on Diversity
5	<ul><li>Social interaction theories.</li></ul>	Focus on Technology
6	<ul><li>Understanding cultural diversity in communication.</li></ul>	Focus on Diversity
7	<ul><li>Understanding cultural diversity in communication.</li><li>Characteristics of language impairments.</li><li>Self-advocacy.</li></ul>	Focus on Technology, Focus on Curriculum and Instruction, Focus on Diversity
10	<ul><li>Understanding cultural diversity in communication.</li><li>Collaboration.</li></ul>	Focus on Technology, Focus on Curriculum and Instruction, Focus on Diversity
Praxis Standards	**Chapter Topics**	**Related Projects or Artifacts**
1	<ul><li>Defining speech and language disorders.</li><li>Characteristics of language impairments.</li></ul>	Focus on Technology
2	<ul><li>Communication disorders as defined by IDEA.</li><li>Nature and extent of services.</li></ul>	Focus on Technology
3	<ul><li>Assistive technology.</li><li>Specialized instructional materials.</li></ul>	

(continued – Standards/Topics – Project Alignment Matrix)

INTASC Principles	Chapter Topics	Related Projects or Artifacts
1	• Understanding typical speech and language development. • Including students with non-disabled peers.	Focus on Technology
2	• Assistive technology. • Understanding limitations.	Focus on Curriculum and Instruction
3	• Including students with communication disorders in the general education curriculum.	Focus on Diversity
4	• Adapting instruction. • Using augmentative and alternative communication systems.	Focus on Curriculum and Instruction
5	• Assistive communication systems and visual supports.	
6	• Typical speech and language development.	Focus on Technology
8	• Evaluating students with communication disorders. • Bilingual evaluation.	
10	• Collaboration.	Focus on Diversity

Materials Available on the Companion Website

Self-quizzes on chapter content

Links to related websites and resources

Links to sample projects or artifacts

Other case study related materials to support comprehensive understanding

Graphic Organizer for Chapter 14

Link to AAC video

Link to Rubristar

Link to the National Information Center for Children and Youth with Disabilities fact sheet on speech and language impairments

Chapter 15
HEARING LOSS

Chapter Overview

Understanding the culture of students with hearing loss is essential for teachers. This understanding will assist educators in holding high expectations for students and including students to the fullest extent. In this chapter students will learn about evaluation, communication, curricular, and assessment strategies that can be utilized in the classroom. It is important to understand the characteristics of hearing loss so that the unique needs of each student can be accommodated while simultaneously providing opportunities for students to learn and grow both socially and academically.

 Don't forget to access the video and audio vignettes that accompany this chapter...

Instructional Goals

After reading this chapter you will be able to:
1. Describe characteristics of students with hearing loss.
2. Recall the major causes of hearing loss.
3. Understand the curricular and instructional needs of students with hearing loss.
4. Describe instructional strategies that lead to successful progression in the general curriculum for students with hearing loss.

Guiding Questions

Don't forget about the Graphic Organizer available on the Companion Website.

How is hearing loss defined?

What are intensity and frequency?

How does terminology change between using a disability-first language and using a people-first language?

What are some characteristics of language and communication for persons who are deaf or hard of hearing?

What are the psychosocial dimensions of deafness or hard of hearing?

What are some causes of low academic achievement among students who are deaf?

List some prelingual causes of hearing loss.

List some postlingual causes of hearing loss.

How are infants evaluated for deafness or hard of hearing?

What are the most common assistive listening devices?

List six factors to consider when thinking about placement and support.

How can curriculum be altered to meet the needs of students who are deaf or have hearing loss?

What is an instructional conversation?

How can understanding the deaf community help you plan curriculum and instruction?

What professionals work with students who are deaf or have hearing loss?

Key Terms
In the space provided below, define the key terms in the chapter.

American Sign Language

Audiologists

Audiometer

Cochlear implants

Diagnostic auditory brain stem response test

Fingerspelling

Interpreters

Manually coded English

Otitis media

Otoacoustic immittance test

Pidgin Sign Language

Prelingual hearing loss

Simultaneous communication

Speech-language pathologist

Case Study and Focus Activity

Case Study Summary

Amala Brown has experienced struggles and successes as a deaf individual. Since elementary school she has attended (in full or in part) public school, where she has used interpreters, real-time captioning, and other related services to help her succeed. Because Amala arrived in the United States at age four, she has had to overcome language barriers while simultaneously learning how to communicate in a non-hearing world. However, she is a very independent and courageous individual who has goals and works to meet those goals on a daily basis.

Focus Activity

Collaboration Connection...	Your Thoughts...
Did the profession of Amala's mother impact her success? Why or why not?	

Diversity Link...	Your Thoughts...
How does Amala's first language impact her success in communicating?	

Focus on Inclusion...	Your Thoughts...
How has Amala interacted with non-disabled peers?	

Universal Design Application...	Your Thoughts...
How has Amala's drive to succeed affected her independence and livelihood?	

Artifact or Project Opportunities

Focus on Diversity:

Read the article "Loneliness in Children with Disabilities: How Teachers Can Help," by Shireen Pavri, published in the Council for Exceptional Children's journal *Teaching Exceptional Children*, Volume 33, Number 6. The article is available online at http://journals.cec.sped.org (a direct hyperlink to the article is available on the Companion Website). Compose a reflection on the article, paying careful attention to how you could embed intervention approaches presented by the authors in Table 2 in your classroom instruction.

Focus on Technology:
Complete a simple search on the Internet for technology resources available to individuals who are deaf or hard of hearing. Write a brief summary of two of the resources, paying careful attention to describing how the technology could be used in the classroom and how it is intended to improve student learning.

Focus on Curriculum and Instruction:
Using a lesson plan available online at the Eisenhower National Clearinghouse (www.enc.org/weblinks/lessonplans), augment the lesson to include necessary accommodations for students who are deaf or hard of hearing. Prepare a new lesson plan that acknowledges the necessary accommodations and makes note of the learning outcomes that should be reached with accommodations in place.

Spot Check

1. How are degrees of hearing loss communicated?

2. What are the major causes of hearing loss?

3. What are key characteristics of student hearing loss?

4. How can a student's academic ability be affected by hearing loss?

Questions and Reflections
(After reading the chapter, use this area to keep track of your questions or reflections.)

⌗Standards/Topics – Project Alignment Matrix

The following professional standards are addressed in Chapter 15 within the correlating chapter topics and with the related projects or artifacts. A comprehensive matrix aligning CEC professional standards, Praxis Standards, and INTASC principles is available in the appendix of the textbook.

CEC Standards	Chapter Topics	Related Projects or Artifacts
1	• Defining hearing loss. • Understanding the process of hearing. • Meeting behavioral needs of students with hearing loss. • Providing related services to support students with hearing loss. • Peer and teacher training and support.	Focus on Collaboration, Focus on Curriculum and Instruction, Focus on Technology
2	• Defining hearing loss. • Understanding the process of hearing. • Meeting behavioral needs of students with hearing loss. • Self-advocacy. • Transitionary services to support independence.	Focus on Collaboration, Focus on Curriculum and Instruction, Focus on Technology
3	• Defining hearing loss. • Meeting behavioral needs of students with hearing loss.	Focus on Technology
4	• Importance of high expectations. • Collaborating to meet the needs of students with hearing loss.	Focus on Technology
5	• Importance of high expectations. • Understanding social needs of students with hearing loss. • Understanding multiple levels of support.	Focus on Curriculum and Instruction and Focus on Diversity
6	• Providing related services to support students with hearing loss. • Transitionary services to support independence.	Focus on Collaboration, Focus on Technology
7	• Importance of high expectations. • Understanding social needs of students with hearing loss. • Peer and teacher training and support. • Understanding multiple levels of support. • Self-advocacy.	Focus on Collaboration, Focus on Curriculum and Instruction, Focus on Technology
8	• Understanding social needs of students with hearing loss. • Providing related services to support students with hearing loss. • Self-advocacy.	Focus on Collaboration, Focus on Technology

(continued – Standards/Topics – Project Alignment Matrix)

	Chapter Topics	Related Projects or Artifacts
9	<ul><li>Providing related services to support students with hearing loss.</li><li>Peer and teacher training and support.</li><li>Collaborating to meet the needs of students with hearing loss.</li><li>Understanding multiple levels of support.</li><li>Transitionary services to support independence.</li></ul>	Focus on Collaboration, Focus on Curriculum and Instruction, Focus on Technology
10	<ul><li>Defining hearing loss.</li><li>Understanding the process of hearing.</li><li>Meeting behavioral needs of students with hearing loss.</li><li>Providing related services to support students with hearing loss.</li><li>Peer and teacher training and support.</li></ul>	Focus on Curriculum and Instruction, Focus on Technology
Praxis Standards	**Chapter Topics**	**Related Projects or Artifacts**
1	<ul><li>Characteristics of hearing loss.</li><li>Causes of hearing loss.</li></ul>	Focus on Curriculum and Instruction
2	<ul><li>Referral processes for students who are deaf or hard of hearing.</li><li>Nature and extent of services.</li></ul>	
3	<ul><li>Assistive technology.</li><li>Specialized instructional materials.</li></ul>	Focus on Technology
INTASC Principles	**Chapter Topics**	**Related Projects or Artifacts**
1	<ul><li>Utilizing American Sign Language, fingerspelling, and other forms of communication.</li><li>Focus on communication.</li></ul>	Focus on Curriculum and Instruction
2	<ul><li>Assistive technology.</li><li>Understanding social needs.</li></ul>	
3	<ul><li>Augmenting curriculum and instruction.</li></ul>	Focus on Curriculum and Instruction, Focus on Diversity
5	<ul><li>Real-time graphic display.</li><li>Using the Internet.</li></ul>	Focus on Technology
6	<ul><li>Assistive technology.</li></ul>	Focus on Technology
8	<ul><li>Evaluating students who have hearing loss.</li><li>Academic versus communication needs.</li></ul>	
9	<ul><li>Understanding the importance of high expectations.</li></ul>	Focus on Curriculum and Instruction
10	<ul><li>Psychological development.</li><li>Collaborating to meet the needs of students with hearing loss.</li></ul>	Focus on Curriculum and Instruction, Focus on Diversity

Materials Available on the Companion Website

Self-quizzes on chapter content

Links to sample projects or artifacts

Link to the National Association of the Deaf (www.nad.org)

Link to the Eisenhower National Clearinghouse (www.enc.org/weblinks/lessonplans)

Other case study related materials to support comprehensive understanding

PowerPoint Presentation for Chapter 15

Graphic Organizer for Chapter 15

Chapter 16
VISUAL IMPAIRMENTS

Chapter Overview

Students with visual impairments account for roughly .04 percent of the total special education population. Even though the presence of these students is not substantial, it is important that educational professionals understand the characteristics, causes, and types of visual impairments. Only with the basic foundational knowledge of visual impairments in place can teachers help their students progress through the general education curriculum. This chapter will present foundational information as well as applicable strategies for meeting the needs of students with visual impairments in the classroom.

 Don't forget to access the video and audio vignettes that accompany this chapter...

Instructional Goals

After reading this chapter you will be able to:
1. Understand the definition and characteristics of students with visual impairments.
2. Recall the assistive technologies available to support appropriate curricular and instructional needs of students with visual impairments.
3. Develop an understanding of the needs of students with visual impairments within the classroom context.
4. Understand how the skills and abilities of students with visual impairments change over time.

Guiding Questions

Don't forget about the Graphic Organizer available on the Companion Website.

What is the legal definition for a visual impairment (including blindness)?

What are the limitations of mobility for students who have visual impairments?

How can the interactions of students be impacted by visual impairments?

What are the major causes of visual impairments?

How does the use of vision interact with the evaluation process?

What is an appropriate reading medium for visually impaired students?

How can assistive technology support students with visual impairments?

What are some examples of specialized instruction and materials that can support students with visual impairments?

How can curriculum be augmented to be attentive to orientation and mobility needs of students who are blind or have low vision?

How does collaboration support students who are blind or have low vision?

Key Terms

In the space provided below, define the key terms in the chapter.

Field of vision

Functionally blind

Legal blindness

Low vision

Self-advocacy

Totally blind

Tunnel vision

Visual acuity

Case Study and Focus Activity

Case Study Summary

Elexis Gillette is a freshman in high school. Elexis has glaucoma and lost his vision early in third grade. He has been strongly encouraged by his mother and his teachers, who maintain high expectations for him as a learner. Elexis puts his best effort into achieving his goals and is positive about making plans for the future. He is accepting of the fact that he cannot do the same things in the same ways as his sighted peers, but asserts that this does not hold him back from participating in activities at school and in the community. He looks forward to a career in technology and is making efforts to independently use the strategies his teachers have taught him over the years.

Focus Activity

Collaboration Connection...	Your Thoughts...
In what ways can a community support individuals who are blind or have low vision?	

Diversity Link...	Your Thoughts...
Would it be appropriate to expect the average community member to be able to assist individuals with blindness or low	

vision when called upon to do so?	
Focus on Inclusion...	**Your Thoughts...**
Can students who are blind or have low vision be completely included in the school environment? Why or why not?	

Universal Design Application...	Your Thoughts...
What would the challenges be in including a student with blindness or low vision in the whole school environment?	

✐ Artifact or Project Opportunities

Focus on Curriculum and Instructional Choices:
Access a WebQuest from the Trackstar system online at http://trackstar.hprtec.org, review the Internet sites within the WebQuest you choose, and rate each site on its attention to the components of Universal Design for Learning. For a refresher on those components review, Chapter 2 or visit the CAST website.

Focus on Collaboration:
Create an autobiography that describes the partners and supports you had in place in order to achieve one goal that you have set and met in your life. Be sure to explain how that goal was developed and achieved; go into as much detail as possible about who supported you and how you were supported in working to achieve that goal.

❓ Spot Check

1. Do individuals who are legally blind have some usable vision?

2. Why is it important to understand how students "use vision"?

3. How can students with visual impairments interact with print media?

4. In what ways do assistive technologies support the learning of students with visual impairments?

5. Why is elementary school a key time for the educational, social, and emotional development of students with visual impairments?

Questions and Reflections
(After reading the chapter, use this area to keep track of your questions or reflections.)

#Standards/Topics – Project Alignment Matrix

The following professional standards are addressed in Chapter 16 within the correlating chapter topics and with the related projects or artifacts. A comprehensive matrix aligning CEC professional standards, Praxis Standards, and INTASC principles is available in the appendix of the textbook.

CEC Standards	Chapter Topics	Related Projects or Artifacts
1	<ul><li>Characteristics of blindness and low vision.</li><li>Legal definitions of blindness.</li><li>Defining visual impairments.</li><li>Limitations of students with blindness or low vision.</li><li>Self-advocacy.</li><li>Limitations in interactions.</li><li>Understanding limitations.</li></ul>	Focus on Collaboration
2	<ul><li>Characteristics of blindness and low vision.</li><li>Legal definitions of blindness.</li><li>Limitations of students with blindness or low vision.</li><li>Orientation and mobility.</li><li>Self-advocacy.</li><li>Understanding limitations.</li></ul>	Focus on Curriculum and Instruction
3	<ul><li>Characteristics of blindness and low vision.</li><li>Limitations of students with blindness or low vision.</li><li>Orientation and mobility.</li><li>Self-advocacy.</li></ul>	Focus on Curriculum and Instruction
4	<ul><li>Self-advocacy.</li></ul>	Focus on Collaboration
5	<ul><li>Self-advocacy.</li><li>Understanding limitations.</li><li>Limitations of students with blindness or low vision.</li><li>Limitations in interactions.</li></ul>	Focus on Curriculum and Instruction
6	<ul><li>Self-advocacy.</li></ul>	Focus on Collaboration
7	<ul><li>Characteristics of blindness and low vision.</li><li>Limitations of students with blindness or low vision.</li><li>Self-advocacy.</li></ul>	Focus on Curriculum and Instruction
8	<ul><li>Self-advocacy.</li></ul>	Focus on Collaboration

(continued – Standards/Topics – Project alignment Matrix)

9	• Legal definitions of blindness. • Limitations of students with blindness or low vision. • Limitations in interactions. • Understanding limitations.	Focus on Curriculum and Instruction, Focus on Collaboration
10	• Collaboration.	
Praxis Standards	**Chapter Topics**	**Related Projects or Artifacts**
1	• Characteristics of blindness and low vision. • Causes of blindness and low vision.	Focus on Collaboration
2	• Legal definitions of blindness. • Nature and extent of services.	
3	• Assistive technology. • Specialized instructional materials.	Focus on Curriculum and Instruction
INTASC Principles	**Chapter Topics**	**Related Projects or Artifacts**
1	• Assistive technology. • Orientation and mobility.	Focus on Curriculum and Instruction
2	• Assistive technology. • Understanding limitations.	
3	• Understanding limitations.	
5	• Self-advocacy.	
6	• Assistive technology.	Focus on Curriculum and Instruction
8	• Evaluating students who have visual impairments.	
10	• Collaboration.	Focus on Collaboration

Materials Available on the Companion Website

Self-quizzes on chapter content

Links to articles for artifact and project opportunities

Links to related websites and resources

Discussion starters

Link to the High Plains Regional Technology in Education Consortium's Trackstar system

Other case study related materials to support comprehensive understanding

PowerPoint Presentation for Chapter 16

Graphic Organizer for Chapter 16

Chapter Specific Graphic Organizers

Remember that each chapter is provided with a Graphic Organizer available in the back of this guide and on the *Companion Website* in digital form. Each Graphic Organizer is designed to focus on the common components including definition/characteristics, identification/ evaluation, curriculum/instruction, and collaboration/teaching. Utilizing the Graphic Organizer in class (during lecture, group work, or independent review) may support your understanding of the multiple levels encompassed by all of the topics being discussed within each chapter. The filing cabinet icon is used to remind you that the Graphic Organizer would be a good companion to that topic or section.

Chapter 1 Overview of Today's Special Education

Definition & Characteristics

Identification & Evaluation

Curriculum & Instruction

Collaboration & Teaching

KEY POINTS, OTHER INFORMATION, RESOURCES, QUESTIONS...

Critical Questions

• Understand the characteristics of special education in today's schools. • Connect individuality with disability in relation to categorization and characteristics. • Identify the categories of disabilities. • Describe the various stakeholders in special education. • Understand the basic components of IDEA.

Chapter 2 Ensuring Progress in the General Curriculum: Universal Design and Inclusion

Definition
&
Characteristics

Identification
&
Evaluation

Curriculum
&
Instruction

Collaboration
&
Teaching

Critical Questions

• Understand how students with disabilities interact within systems of accountability. • Reflect on how the use of a universally designed learning experience can support students with exceptionalities and contribute to the overall quality of curriculum and instruction. • Differentiate among various placement options for students with disabilities. • Recall the key characteristics of inclusion. • Understand why progressing through the general

KEY POINTS, OTHER INFORMATION, RESOURCES, QUESTIONS...

Chapter 3 Ensuring Progress in the General Education Curriculum: Collaboration and Multicultural Responsiveness

```
     ⎛ Definition ⎞        ⎛ Identification ⎞        ⎛ Curriculum ⎞        ⎛ Collaboration ⎞
     ⎜     &      ⎟        ⎜      &         ⎟        ⎜     &      ⎟        ⎜      &        ⎟
     ⎝Characteristics⎠     ⎝  Evaluation    ⎠        ⎝Instruction ⎠        ⎝  Teaching     ⎠
```

Critical Questions

• Describe how collaboration can enable students with disabilities to progress in the general curriculum. • Discuss the various stakeholders in collaboration. • Identify effective approaches to collaboration. • Describe the process involved in creating collaborative teams. • Connect multicultural responsiveness with student success in the general curriculum. • Describe how culture can influence roles and expectations in collaborative teams.

KEY POINTS, OTHER INFORMATION, RESOURCES, QUESTIONS...

Chapter 4 Learning Disabilities:
Disorder in one or more of the basic psychological processes…

Definition & Characteristics

Identification & Evaluation

Curriculum & Instruction

Collaboration & Teaching

Critical Questions

- Describe characteristics of a learning disability. • Discuss and understand the basic components of the universally designed curriculum.
- Recognize the importance of student progress with the general curriculum. • Understand the benefits of collaboration and communication across settings. • Connect knowledge to specific case studies. • Create lesson plans that augment instructional and curriculum choices to insure the

KEY POINTS, OTHER INFORMATION, RESOURCES, QUESTIONS…

Chapter 5 Emotional or Behavioral Disorders:
Characterized by behavioral or emotional responses…

Definition & Characteristics

Identification & Evaluation

Curriculum & Instruction

Collaboration & Teaching

Critical Questions

- Describe the characteristics of emotional or behavioral disorders. • Understand the importance of collaboration in working with students with emotional or behavioral disorders. • Understand the differences between biological and environmental influences. • Understand how to effectively adapt assessments for students with emotional or behavioral disorders.
  - Utilize basic approaches to effectively adapt assessments for students with emotional or behavioral disorders.

KEY POINTS, OTHER INFORMATION, RESOURCES, QUESTIONS…

Chapter 6 Attention-Deficit/Hyperactivity Disorder:
A persistent pattern of inattention and/or hyperactivity-impulsivity…

Definition & Characteristics

Identification & Evaluation

Curriculum & Instruction

Collaboration & Teaching

Critical Questions

- Identify causes of AD/HD. ● Understand the complexities of AD/HD in relation to providing services for students under the IDEA.
- Recall the subtypes of AD/HD provided by the American Psychiatric Association. ● Describe positive traits associated with AD/HD.
- Understand the social, emotional, and behavioral needs of students with AD/HD.
- Describe how curricular and instructional choices can be augmented to meet the needs of students with AD/HD.

KEY POINTS, OTHER INFORMATION, RESOURCES, QUESTIONS…

High performance capabilities that require service or activities...

Definition & Characteristics

Identification & Evaluation

Curriculum & Instruction

Collaboration & Teaching

Critical Questions

- Understand the role of giftedness within special education. • Apply knowledge of Universal Design for Learning to the curriculum and instruction for gifted education. • Recall the behavioral and social characteristics of students identified as gifted or talented.
  - Reflect on the benefits of collaboration in supporting the education of students identified as gifted or talented.

KEY POINTS, OTHER INFORMATION, RESOURCES, QUESTIONS...

Chapter 8 Mental Retardation:

Characterized by significant limitations both in intellectual functioning and in adaptive behavior...

Definition & Characteristics

Identification & Evaluation

Curriculum & Instruction

Collaboration & Teaching

Critical Questions

- Define characteristics of mental retardation. ● Describe different supports that may collaborate to meet the needs of students with mental retardation. ● Describe different characteristics of mental retardation.
- Understand the differences among biomedical, social, behavioral, and educational causes of mental retardation. ● Begin to understand different assessments that are used to evaluate students with mental retardation. ● Define self-determinat...

KEY POINTS, OTHER INFORMATION, RESOURCES, QUESTIONS...

Chapter 9 Severe and Multiple Disabilities:
No single definition covers all of the associated conditions…

Definition
&
Characteristics

Identification
&
Evaluation

Curriculum
&
Instruction

Collaboration
&
Teaching

Critical Questions

- Define severe and multiple disabilities. • What are five major themes associated with the successful inclusion of students with severe disabilities? • Describe the MAPS process. • Define partial participation as it relates to students with severe and multiple disabilities.
- Recall how peer tutoring can support students with disabilities.

KEY POINTS, OTHER INFORMATION, RESOURCES, QUESTIONS…

Chapter 10 Autism:

Developmental disability that effects verbal, nonverbal, and social...

Definition & Characteristics

Identification & Evaluation

Curriculum & Instruction

Collaboration & Teaching

Critical Questions

- Describe characteristics of autism. ● Discuss and understand how autism is identified and what causes have been linked to autism. ● Discuss and understand how autism is identified in the classroom and larger community. ● Understand the benefits of collaboration and communication across settings. ● Connect knowledge to specific case studies. ● Discuss and understand how instructional and curricular choices can support students with autism in progressing through the general education curriculum.

KEY POINTS, OTHER INFORMATION, RESOURCES, QUESTIONS...

Chapter 7 Other Health Impairments.

Limited strength, vitality or alertness, including a heightened alertness to environmental stimuli....

```
┌─────────────┐   ┌─────────────┐   ┌─────────────┐   ┌─────────────┐
│ Definition  │   │Identification│  │ Curriculum  │   │Collaboration│
│     &       │   │     &       │   │     &       │   │     &       │
│Characteristics│  │ Evaluation  │   │ Instruction │   │  Teaching   │
└─────────────┘   └─────────────┘   └─────────────┘   └─────────────┘
```

KEY POINTS, OTHER INFORMATION, RESOURCES, QUESTIONS....

Critical Questions

- Describe characteristics of Other Health Impairments. ● Understand the causes of Other Health Impairments. ● Describe evaluation processes for students with Other Health Impairments. ● Reflect on the importance of inclusion for students with Other Health Impairments. ● Understand the curricular and instructional needs.

Chapter 12 Physical Disabilities:

Orthopedic impairment affecting a child's educational performance...

Definition & Characteristics

Identification & Evaluation

Curriculum & Instruction

Collaboration & Teaching

Critical Questions

- Understand the prevalence of physical disabilities. ● Describe how students with physical disabilities can be evaluated. ● Understand how students with disabilities can be included in
- Reflect on the assistive technologies available to support communication and mobility. ● Understand how students with disabilities can be included in the general education curriculum.

KEY POINTS, OTHER INFORMATION, RESOURCES, QUESTIONS...

Chapter 13 Traumatic Brain Injury.

Caused by an external force resulting in total or partial functional or psychosocial...

Definition & Characteristics

Identification & Evaluation

Curriculum & Instruction

Collaboration & Teaching

KEY POINTS, OTHER INFORMATION, RESOURCES, QUESTIONS...

Critical Questions

- Describe how traumatic brain injury can affect a student's social, academic, and emotional abilities. ● Recall effective teaching practices for working with students with traumatic brain injury. ● Understand how to encourage participation.
  - ● Describe strategies that would be helpful to the transition of students with TBI.

Chapter 14 Communication Disorders:
The components of the process affected, speech, and language…

Definition & Characteristics

Identification & Evaluation

Curriculum & Instruction

Collaboration & Teaching

Critical Questions

• Describe how students with communication disorders are supported in the general education curriculum.
• Understand cultural diversity in communication. • Reflect on how communication disorders can be accommodated in the general curriculum.
• Describe the role of a speech language pathologist in evaluating students with communication disorders.

KEY POINTS, OTHER INFORMATION, RESOURCES, QUESTIONS…

Chapter 15 Hearing Loss:

A hearing loss that is severe enough to affect educational performance....

```
Definition          Identification        Curriculum          Collaboration
    &                    &                    &                    &
Characteristics     Evaluation           Instruction          Teaching
```

KEY POINTS, OTHER INFORMATION, RESOURCES, QUESTIONS...

Critical Questions

- Describe characteristics of students with hearing loss. ● Recall the major causes of hearing loss.
- Understand the curricular and instructional needs of students with a hearing loss.
- Describe instructional strategies that lead to successful progression in the general curriculum for students with hearing loss.

Chapter 16 Visual Impairments:

Impairment in vision that adversely affects educational performance...

Definition & Characteristics

Identification & Evaluation

Curriculum & Instruction

Collaboration & Teaching

Critical Questions

● Understand the definition and characteristics of students with visual impairments. ● Recall the assistive technologies available to support appropriate curricular and instructional needs of students with visual impairments. ● Develop an understanding of the needs of students with visual impairments within the classroom context. ● Understand how the skills and abilities of students with visual impairments change over time.

KEY POINTS, OTHER INFORMATION, RESOURCES, QUESTIONS...